# 100 WALKS IN
# County Durham

The Crowood Press

First published in 1992 by
The Crowood Press Ltd
Ramsbury,
Marlborough
Wiltshire SN8 2HR

www.crowood.com

This impression 2004

**British Library Cataloguing-in-Publication Data**
A catalogue record for this book is
available from the British Library

ISBN 1-85233-5217

All maps by Sharon Perks

Cover picture by John Cleare

Typeset by Carreg Limited, Ross-on-Wye, Herefordshire

Printed in Great Britain by CPI Bath

# THE CONTRIBUTORS

John Bennington

Helen Blenkhorn

Charles Emett

Simon Holloway

Brenda Whitelock

# CONTENTS

36. Flatts Wood $4^1/_2$m (7km)
37. Middleton-in-Teesdale and Wythes Hill 5m (8km)
38. St John's Chapel and Middlehope Shield Mine 5m (8km)
39. Lumley Park and Castle 5m (8km)
40. The Prince Bishops Circular 5m (8km)
41. Middleton-in-Teesdale and Hudeshope Valley 6m (9.5km)
42. Middleton-in-Teesdale and Mickleton 6m (9.5km)
43. Cotherstone and Baldersdale 6m (9.5km)
44. Middleton-One-Row and Newsham Hall 6m (9.5km)
45. Wolsingham and Tunstall 6m (9.5km)
46. High and Low Coniscliffe $6^1/_4$m (10km)
47. Cockfield Fell $6^1/_4$m (10km)
48. Winston and Old Richmond $6^1/_2$m (10km)
49. The Coniscliffes $6^1/_2$m (10km)
50. Forest Teesdale $6^1/_2$m (10km)
51. Croft to Middleton-One-Row $6^1/_2$m (10km)
52. Castle Eden Dene 7m (11km)
53. Brignall Banks 7m (11km)
54. Barnard Castle and Boldron 7m (11km)
55. Barnard Castle, Flatts Wood and Cotherstone 7m (11km)
56. Barnard Castle and Lartington 7m (11km)
57. Middleton-in-Teesdale and Hardberry Hill 7m (11km)
58. Romaldkirk and Cotherstone 7m (11km)
59. Lower Baldersdale 7m (11km)
60. St John's Chapel and Cowshill 7m (11km)
61. Sunderland Bridge and Shincliffe 7m (11km)
62. Staindrop and Streatlam Park Wall 7m (11km)
63. Bowes and God's Bridge $7^1/_2$m (12km)
64. Westgate and St John's Chapel $7^1/_2$m (12km)
65. Bowes and Pasture End $7^1/_2$m (12km)
66. Bowes and Sleightholme Circular $7^1/_2$m (12km)
67. Durham City's Medieval Pilgrim Walk $7^1/_2$m (12km)
68. The Lanchester Valley Railway Walk 8m (13km)
69. ...and longer version 10m (16km)
70. Wolsingham and Tunstall Reservoir 8m (13km)
71. St John's Chapel and Burnhope Reservoir 8m (13km)
72. Bowlees and the Green Trod 8m (13km)

73. Hamsterley Forest and High Acton 8m (13km)

74. Middleton-in-Teesdale and Hardberry Gutter 8m (13km)

75. Nanny Mayor's Incline 8m (13km)

76. Staindrop, Cockfield and Evenwood 8m (13km)

77. Monk's Moor 8m (13km)

78. Widdybank Fell 8m (13km)

79. Stanhope Dene and Crawley Edge 8m (13km)

80. Sherburn and Pittington Circular 9m (14.5km)

81. Summerhouse and Hilton 9m (14.5km)

82. Burnhope Burn 9m (14.5km)

83. Cotherstone and the River Balder 9m (14.5km)

84. Hury Reservoir and Birk Hat 9m (14.5km)

85. Langleydale Common and Woodland Fell 9m (14.5km)

86. Meeting of the Waters 9m (14.5km)

87. Bishop Auckland and Page Bank 9m (14.5km)

88. Brandon to Bishop Auckland $9^1/_2$m (15km)

89. Barningham Moor 10m (16km)

90. The Upper Teesdale Waterfalls 10m (16km)

91. Elephant Trees 10m (16km)

92. The River Balder 10m (16km)

93. Killhope Wheel and Allenheads 10m (16km)

94. Rookhope and Redburn Common 10m (16km)

95. The Derwent Railway $10^1/_2$m (17km)

96. Sunderland Bridge and Whitworth Road 11m (17.5km)

97. The Deerness and Lanchester Valleys 11m (17.5km)

98. The Vale of Harwood 11m (17.5km)

99. Cronkley Fell 12m (19km)

100. Stanhope, Eastgate and Rookhope 13m (21km)

# INTRODUCTION

The Crowood Press are greatly indebted to our contributors who walked cheerfully all over the county researching the walks for this book. It must be borne in mind that while all the details of these walks (hedges, fences, stiles, and so on) were correct at the time of going to print, the countryside is constantly changing and we cannot be held responsible if details in the walk descriptions are found to be inaccurate. We would be grateful if walkers would let us know of any major alterations to the walks described so that we may incorporate any changes in future editions. Please write to THE 100 WALKS SERIES, The Crowood Press, Crowood Lane, Ramsbury, Marlborough, Wiltshire SN8 2HR. Walkers are strongly advised to take with them the relevant map for the area and Ordnance Survey maps are recommended for each walk. The walks are listed by length - from approximately 2 miles to 13 miles. No attempt has been made to estimate how long the walks will take as this can vary so greatly depending on the strength and fitness of the walkers and the time spent exploring the points of interest highlighted. Nearly all the walks are circular and the majority offer a recommended place to seek refreshments. Telephone numbers of these pubs and cafés are included in case you want to check on opening times, meals available, and so on.

We hope you enjoy exploring the county of Durham in the best possible way - on foot - and ask that you cherish its beautiful places by always remembering the country code:

Enjoy the country and respect its life and work
Guard against all risk of fire
Fasten all gates
Keep dogs under close control
Keep to public footpaths across all farmland
Use gates and stiles to cross field boundaries
Leave all livestock, machinery and crops alone
Take your litter home
Help to keep all water clean
Protect wildlife, plants and trees
Make no unnecessary noise

**Good walking.**

County Durham

North
Sea

2/3
32    40
20

95        39

82

93        94        14
                     75
         79  100     68/69
                      97        37
    60  38            45 70 67
71      64

98                              Durham    16  30
78  50      24     41  80  57    17  33  80  35  6  91
99      72  4  22  23  77  73  12  18        34  29
    10                      11              61        52
              42        85        47              96
         58        1   59
                 83
         84     43        76    27  25  62  8
Barnard        48  9  21  7
Castle     36  56  55  54
92                              Bishop
                               Auckland  15  26  28
         19  63  86                      88  87
         65  66        53              81        Darlington
                      89              49
                                      46
                                      51  44
                                        31

# Walk 1    COTHERSTONE AND HALLGARTH HILL    2m (3km)

Maps: OS Sheets Landranger 92; Outdoor Leisure 31.

*A short, but lovely, walk.*

Start: The Fox and Hounds, Cotherstone.

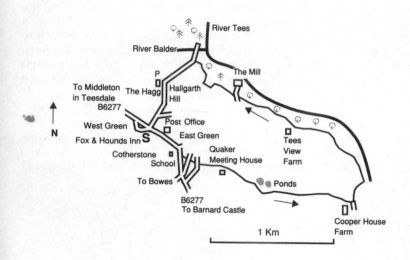

From the Fox and Hounds, on **Cotherstone's** West Green, go along the main street past the post office and the school to the East Green. Cross the stream to go along a path between the houses lining the green. The path leads to a back lane: cross this to enter a field through a gate. Continue close to the left side of the field to reach the Quaker Meeting House. Go over two stone stiles and cross another field, keeping to the right of some ponds. On reaching a small stream, go left along its bank to a bridge. Cross and continue along a narrow path to a stile. Cross and bear left. Cross two fields to reach another stile in a wall. Keep straight ahead, edging a wood on the left, and, ignoring a stile in a facing wall over to your right, continue to a gap in the same wall close to where it meets the end of the wood. Go through this gap and continue close to the wall on your left to reach a grassy track close to the buildings of Cooper House Farm. Turn left down a slope to a stile just short of the stream, from where there is a lovely view of the River Tees over to your right. Cross the stream, bear left up the slope and go along the left side of the wood. Do not enter the fields to the left. Just past the farm the path joins a track. Follow this along the edge of a steep wooded slope that runs along the bank of the River Tees. Where the track bends left, go ahead through a small gate and along a grassy track to another gate. Beyond, cross another track and follow a pleasant green track with the river and an old mill below and on the right. Pass **Abraham Hilton's** tombstone, and cross a stile into a field. Pass some sheds to reach a gate. Go through, turn right and descend some steps. There is a magnificent view of the River Tees just below its confluence with the Balder from here. The steps lead to a road: turn left through an open public area called The Hagg. Towering on your left is Hallgarth Hill, the site of a 12th-century castle which was the home of the medieval lords of Cotherstone, the Fitzhughs. The road will bring you back to the village opposite the Fox and Hounds.

## POINTS OF INTEREST:
**Cotherstone** – The village has been an agricultural community since Anglo-Saxon times. Cotherstone Cheese is still made locally.
**Abraham Hilton** – The founder of several local charities. He died in 1902 aged 87 years.

## REFRESHMENTS:
*The Fox and Hounds*, Cotherstone (tel no: 0833 50241).
*The Red Lion*, Cotherstone (tel no: 0833 50236).

## Walks 2 & 3  DIPTON, PONTOP PIKE AND LOW EWEHURST  2m (3km) or 5m (8km)

Maps: OS Sheets Landranger 88; Pathfinder NZ 05/15.

*Two relatively short walks that can be completed as a single outing.*

Start: At 154536, the car park, Dipton.

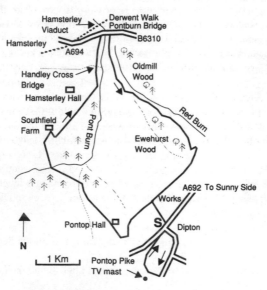

From the car park cross the A692 and go along Cooperative Terrace. Where the road turns left, continue along Pontop Pike Lane and turn right along a concrete road to derelict Pontop Pike Farm. As you turn right at the ruin the tall T.V. transmitter mast towers ahead. Pass the station buildings and continue northwards on to Pontop Pike Fell, from where there are good views all round. At the trig point take the centre path, downhill, into a wood. Turn right along a tarmac path to just beyond Tennyson Gardens and turn left to reach the main street. Turn right to rejoin the car park. For the second walk go 20 yards beyond the car park and turn left at a Scout H.Q. to take a downhill path alongside some allotments and enter a field through a kissing gate. Cross the field and turn left along an embankment path. Cross Pikeshaw Burn on a footbridge.

14

Continue half-left along a stiled path, then right to join a farm track in front of **Pontop Hall Farm**. Once past the farm go right, over a stile, and cross three stiled fields to enter Pontop Low Wood. Bear right along a path that soon becomes a woodland drive. Continue along it as it swings first left and downhill, then right and uphill before dropping again to an opening. About 100 yards beyond this, take the path on your right to South Burn and cross it on some sunken stepping stones. Turn left, upstream, and in a few yards·turn right, uphill, through the wood to exit under a pylon, crossing a waymarked stile beside a gate. Follow the path along two sides of the field to Southfield Farm, where turn right along a farm road, then go left at a 'Public Byway' signpost. Go in a north-easterly direction across stiled fields to enter Hamsterley Hall grounds. Continue along the path to join a drive near some waterfalls. Go over **Handley Cross Bridge** and take the main drive to a kissing gate on the left of the lodge gates. Go through it on to the B6310 and turn right over Pontburn Bridge. Keep on the road for 30 yards, to where a 'Public Footpath' signpost on your right directs you over a footbridge into Oldmill Wood. Go left along a path out of the wood and into some fields. Go half-left along the edge of a field at first and then a wood. Go across two fields to exit just before Low Ewehurst Farm. At the farm turn left along an unsurfaced lane. Where the lane bends for the second time leave it over a stile near a gate on your right. Cross the field ahead on a cart track and stay with it as it climbs through the wood. When the cart track bears right and ceases, continue along a path out of the wood to reach an enclosed path. Turn right along a level path and cross stiled fields to reach the outward route. Turn left along it, back to Dipton.

## POINTS OF INTEREST:
**Pontop Hall Farm** – The building served as a Roman Catholic Seminary between 1794 and 1795.
**Handley Cross Bridge** – The bridge was named after the book *Handley Cross* by Robert S Surtees.

## REFRESHMENTS:
There are pubs and a café in Dipton.

# Walk 4          BOWLEES AND HOLWICK          2¹/₂m (4km)

Maps: OS Sheets Landranger 92; Outdoor Leisure 31.

*A smashing little walk visiting two lovely Teesdale villages.*

Start: The Bowlees Picnic Area Car Park.

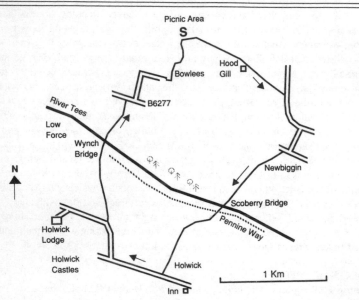

From the car park pass behind the wardens hut, cross a cattle grid and continue uphill along a farm track. Where the track bends left leave it, going straight ahead. Bear right towards a gateway at the end of the wall ahead. Go through the gate and continue close to the right side of a field. Go through a gate at the back of a row of houses at Hood Gill and continue past a barn on your left. Go uphill to a stone stile. Beyond, bear right to another stile, beside a gate, on to a minor road. Go right, into Newbiggin and, where the road bifurcates, go right, along a narrow road to reach the B6277 after about ¹/₄ mile. Cross the road and go over a stile beside a gate. Cross the meadow ahead diagonally right along a clear path to a corner stile and continue across two more fields to the River Tees which is crossed over Scoberry Bridge. Hereabouts, in summer, there are common sandpipers and spotted flycatchers.

Briefly join the Pennine Way, turning right, along it, but almost at once go left over a stile in a fence and continue diagonally right across a meadow to another stile in a wall on your right. Cross this and turn left, aiming for a barn which you pass on your left. Continue up the slope ahead and cross a stile leading on to a minor road in the village of **Holwick**. Turn right and after about $1/_2$ mile, where it curves sharply right, look ahead for a lovely view of the wooded banks of the river Tees. The large building in its own grounds on your left is Holwick Lodge which was built in the late 10th century for Cosmo Bonsor M.P., who had leased the grouse shooting from the Earl of Strathmore. Today the house is still used by shooting parties.

Where the road curves left towards Holwick Lodge continue straight ahead across a field to a stile in the facing wall. Go over and bear left towards another stile in the bottom left corner of the next field. Cross a small stone bridge to reach the Pennine Way. Go over the Way and the Wynch Bridge (see Note to Walk 10) from where there are splendid views of Low Force upstream. Continue long the path through trees, go through a 'squeeze' stile and cross two fields to the B6277. Cross and go along the minor road opposite to the Bowlees Visitor Centre. Take the path alongside the Centre to the picnic area car park.

POINTS OF INTEREST:
**Holwick** – Until 1974, when the county boundary was changed, Holwick was the most northerly village in Yorkshire.

REFRESHMENTS:
*The Strathmore Arms*, Holwick (tel no: 0833 40362).

## Walk 5  MIDDLETON-IN-TEESDALE AND THE RIVER TEES  2¹/₂m (4km)

Maps: OS Sheets Landranger 92; Outdoor Leisure 31.

*A little gem of a walk, waymarked with yellow arrows.*

Start: The Memorial Fountain, Middleton-in-Teesdale.

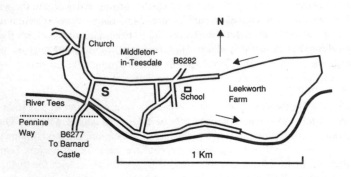

Turn left into Bridge Street and go along it towards the bridge over the River Tees. The bridge was built in 1811, with money from public subscription, to replace an earlier structure. The new bridge collapsed during its erection. Richard Atlee, a butcher had frequently predicted its fall and at the time of the catastrophe he happened to be pointing out its imperfections to his wife when they were buried in debris and killed. Go left along a riverside path just before the bridge. The cobbled surface of the riverside path suggests that it was once well used: lead miners walked to work and some would have used this path. Soon a small building on the riverbank is passed: it is a gauging station used by the Northumbrian Water Authority for recording the water flow in the river. The row of terraced houses on your left used to be the homes of employees of the London Lead Company. The path continues along the riverside, going past a low

18

stone wall in the riverbank, opposite an attractive small beechwood. Continue along the edge of two fields, passing Leekworth Farm with its characteristic arched barn over on your left. Cross a stile into a field which, in summer, contains caravans, and go over another stile as the river makes a large bend to the left. Along this stretch of water that slalom canoe racing takes place: dippers and, in summer, sandpipers can be seen on the river's rocky outcrops. Go along a narrow section of path above rocks and turn left at the end of a stone wall. Bear right across a field to a stile in another stone wall. Continue along the next field edge to a waymarker post. There turn left along the line of the field furrow to the right of a black barn. Go straight across the field to a stile, and then bear slightly left and down to another stile into the next field. Continue towards the corner of a wall, cross a small flagstone bridge and, keeping the wall to your right, go to a stile alongside a gate. Cross and go along the road ahead, through a housing estate. When the main road, the B6282, is reached at a tangent, keep going straight ahead to the car park and **Middleton's** handsome cast iron fountain from where you started.

POINTS OF INTEREST:
**Middleton-in-Teesdale** – The town is the main centre for Upper Teesdale and developed largely as a result of the lead mining industry. It was here that the Quaker owned London Lead Mining Company established its North of England headquarters in 1815. The prominent furrows passed en route are the result of ancient farming. From them, to the left, there is a fine view of Upper Teesdale, with the distinctive wooded knoll of Kirk Carrion – site of an ancient burial mound and reputedly haunted – in the distance.

REFRESHMENTS:
Hotels, pubs and cafés in Middleton-in-Teesdale.

**DURHAM PENINSULA**

Maps: OS Sheets Landranger 88; Pathfinder NZ 24/34.

*An easy walk with gradual ascents, crossing two of Durham's five bridges.*

Start: Durham Market Place.

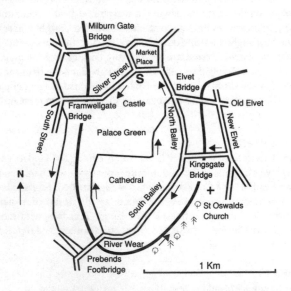

Cars may be parked in Milburngate car park a short step from the Market Place.

Leave the Market Place by Silver Street, a pedestrian way. Cross Framwellgate Bridge, built by Bishop Ralph Flambard in 1128; the ancient bridge is a good place to view, and perhaps photograph, the cathedral and the castle. At the west end of the bridge descend the steps to a riverside path. Follow the path of the weir, at each side of which is an old mill. From here there is a beautiful view, which includes the cathedral, the river weir and the old corn mill. Walk behind Bishop's Mill to reach Prebends' Bridge, and pause there to read Sir Walter Scott's poem, which is inscribed at the end of the bridge. It begins:

> *Grey towers of Durham*
> *Yet well I loved thy mixed and massive piles.*

Cross the footbridge if you wish to admire the views up and down the river: it is worth crossing to view a modern sculpture depicting the Last Supper – recross the bridge to continue the walk.

Continue along the path known as 'The Banks' which is owned and carefully preserved by the Dean and Chapter of Durham. The path climbs gradually to come out by the 12th century **St Oswald's Church**. Walk through the churchyard and continue down Church Street into and along New Elvet. Turn left to Kingsgate Bridge, a modern bridge, built in 1963. Cross the bridge to The Peninsula, climb steps and enter Bow Lane. Pass the ancient church of St Mary-le-Bow and St Chad's College to reach the Bailey. Turn left along South Bailey passing St John's College, built in 1730, top reach, at the end, Watergate, an archway. Walk under the archway, but do not take the road down to Prebends' Bridge. Instead, turn right and follow the wooded path below the old City Walls. Where the path divides, take the higher path, passing the western end of the cathedral to reach the New Library. Turn right and ascend the narrow Windy Gap, passing the home of John Meade Faulkner (1858–1932) to reach the **Palace Green**. From Palace Green walk down Owengate into Sadler Street and on into the Market Place.

POINTS OF INTEREST:
**St Oswald's Church** – A fine 12th century parish church. The grounds are kept in remarkably good order, with a fine selection of mature trees, and is rich in gravestones. Viewing of the church is restricted: Weekdays 11am–3pm, Sundays 2pm–3pm, plus service times. The restriction is a result of a fire in 1984. There is a Bell Ringing Day, usually held in September.
**Palace Green** – Time should be allowed to explore the historic buildings around Palace Green. Bishops Cosin's Hall and Library, the University Library, Abbey House and the old Grammar School, the Almshouses, the Cathedral and the Castle.

REFRESHMENTS:
There is a coffee shop opposite St Oswald's Church (tel no: 091 386 0222).
There is also an abundance of coffee shops, pubs and restaurants in the centre of Durham.

# Walk 7    BARNARD CASTLE AND TOWLER HILL    3m (5km)

Maps: OS Sheets Landranger 92; Outdoor Leisure 31.

*A most pleasant walk along the west bank of the River Tees.*

Start: Scar Top, near the castle, Barnard Castle.

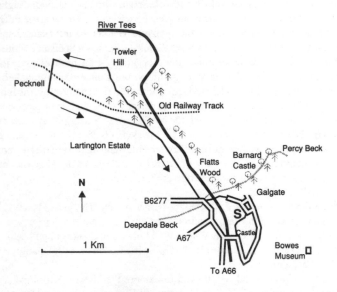

From the information board on Scar Top, from where, on your left, the wall of the 12th century castle are clearly seen, take the wide tarmac path on your right, going between children's swings and a paddling pool. Continue along it, descending to the River Tees in Flatts Wood, and cross the river on an aqueduct-cum-footbridge, from where there are fine views of the castle. Once across the bridge, turn right along the Middleton-in-Teesdale road. Very shortly, after going past a cottage, go right, through a kissing gate and along a most pleasant track, close to the River Tees on your right. After ¹/₂ mile cross a cattle grid and a small stream, before passing a cottage on your right. Stay on the track for a further 50 yards beyond the cottage, and at a waymarked post go right, along a narrow, grassy path which climbs through a stand of Norwegian Spruce to the trackbed of the former Barnard Castle to Kirkby Stephen railway line.

    Cross the trackbed to a stile. Cross and go ahead close to the right side of a field to a stile in a facing hedge. Cross and go over the field ahead close to its left side, to reach, after 300 yards, another stile. Cross to join a farm track leading towards the farm buildings of **Towler Hill Farm**. Stay on the track as it bends sharp left just short of the farm buildings, and continue for $^1/_4$ mile between large, open fields. At two oak trees the track again bends left: do likewise, going through two gates and under the old railway line into a field backed by woodland. Stay on the track along the right side of the field as far as the entrance to the buildings beyond the stone wall at Pechnell. Now turn left along the track towards the cottage, and skirt the left boundary fence and wall. Cross a field towards some telegraph poles, aiming for a distant white gate. Go through the gate into a small plantation. The grassy path beyond soon joins a broad track: go ahead, along it. The track goes downhill to where you branched right on the outward section, close to the cottage near the River Tees. Here turn right and re-trace your steps to Scar Top.

## POINTS OF INTEREST:
**Towler Hill Farm** – It was from near Towler Hill Farm that the famous English painter J M W Turner painted a view of Barnard Castle in 1816. This was one of many views he recorded on his travels through the area.

## REFRESHMENTS:
Hotels, pubs and cafés in Barnard Castle.

Walk 8　　**Staindrop and Snotterton Hall**　　3m (5km)

Maps: OS Sheets Landranger 92; Pathfinder NZ 12/13.

*A very pleasant walk across fields and along quiet country lanes.*

Start: Staindrop Post Office.

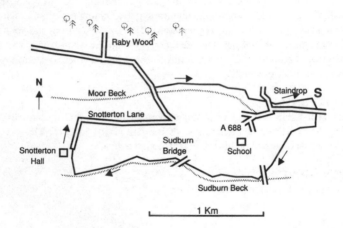

From the post office cross the road and the village green and go down the narrow lane next to Scarth Hall. At the bottom of the lane turn right to a stile and then bear left across the large field ahead. Go through a gate, cross a stone bridge and bear slightly right to a stile in the hedge opposite. Cross and go towards a double telegraph pole and on to a stile in a stone wall. Cross this, and the minor road beyond, to another stile. Beyond this, continue alongside Sudburn Beck, going through nine small, narrow fields. After about $\frac{1}{2}$ mile, climb some steps to reach the main A688 road at Sudburn Bridge. Cross with care, and go over the old road to a stone stile. Keep close to Sudburn Beck as it bends left. Soon a gate in a stone wall is reached just below the white painted buildings of Snotterton Hall on your right. Go through the gate ahead to reach a footbridge over Sudburn Beck. Do not cross the bridge. Instead, turn right, up the field and go through a gate into the farmyard of Snotterton Hall. Keeping to the right of the buildings continue along the farm road from where the views, especially across the lower lying land ahead and to the east, are particularly lovely. The tower of Staindrop church (see Note to Walk 25) is seen in the distance. Soon the farm road turns sharp right to become Snotterton Lane. After $^1/_2$ mile the lane joins the B6279, the main Moor Road, meeting it at a tangent at Morton House, where the road bends. Cross the road and turn left along it to reach the point where it crosses Moor Beck. Immediately over the bridge go right, over a wooden stile, and continue along the beckside. Leave the first field over a wooden stile. Cross a second field and leave over a step stile in a wall. Continue close to a hedge on your right across a third field, continuing into another field where, almost at once, you turn right, through a small gap in the hedge on your right. Now follow a narrow path known locally as 'knicky nack' to reach the corner of North Green in Staindrop (see Note to Walk 27). Go through the village, so returning to the post office.

REFRESHMENTS:
*The Wheatsheaf Inn*, Staindrop (tel no: 0833 60280).

Walk 9    **BARNARD CASTLE AND ABBEY BRIDGE**    3m (5km)
Maps: OS Sheets Landranger 92; Outdoor Leisure 31.
*A gentle, riverside walk.*
Start: Scar Top, near the Castle, Barnard Castle.

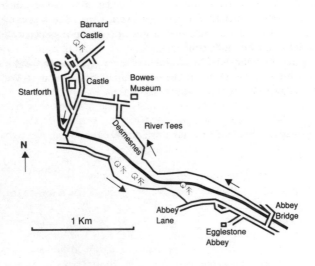

From the information board on Scar Top go left across a grassed area towards the castle (see Note to Walk 36). When you are close to the entrance turn right along a path that descends steeply to reach the River Tees where the **County Bridge** spans it. Do not cross the bridge, but go left, along Bridgegate, for about 250 yards to the Blue Bell pub on the corner. Turn right along Thorngate, an attractive street with some fine, restored houses. Continue over the footbridge that spans the Tees just below a bend, and go up the steep path ahead. Turn left at the top and go along a path at first, and then a road. At the end cross a stone stile and bear right through a caravan site along a tarmac road that goes slightly uphill along an avenue of trees. Just before you reach the trees, cross a stile in the fence on your left and go over four stiled fields, staying close to a hedge on your left, and with the river below. Bowes Museum and Barnard Castle school can be seen from here.

Exit the fourth field by way of a stone stile on to a narrow lane. Go left, downhill, and cross the 17th century Bow Bridge over Thorsgill Beck. Continue along the lane close to the Tees on your left, passing **Egglestone Abbey** on higher ground to your right. About $1/_4$ mile past the Abbey entrance turn left to cross the lovely Abbey Bridge, which bridges the Tees as it flows through a gorge. At the far side go through a small gap in the wall on our left and follow a path through woodland along the north bank of the river. On reaching a wooden stile cross into a field and keep close to the riverbank for $1/_4$ mile, passing through several gates and going along a path with a high fence on the right. Where the fencing ends, cross a stile next to a gate and bear right across a field, heading towards a stone building.

Before reaching the building turn right up a sloping field to reach a stile near a metal gate in a wall. Cross and follow a path diagonally left over a grassy space known as The Desmesnes. Skirt the pitches on your left, and make for a distant gate beside a stone wall. Go through and enter a high-walled lane on the right through a kissing gate. The lane will bring you into Newgate, near the Bowes Museum: turn left, along Newgate, to the 17th century Market Cross building. Go right, along the main street, back to Galgate, your starting point.

## POINTS OF INTEREST:

**County Bridge** – The bridge was built in 1569, and until 1974 was on the Yorkshire-Durham border.

**Egglestone Abbey** – Ralph de Multon founded the Abbey of St Mary and St John the Baptist in 1196 for the Premonstratersian order of Regular Canons.

The remains of a paper mill can be seen on the south bank of the Tees near the Abbey. Paper was laid out to dry on the rocks beside the river. Turner painted both the mill and the Abbey in the early 19th century when the mill was still working.

## REFRESHMENTS:

Hotels, pubs and cafés in Barnard Castle.

# Walk 10    LOW FORCE AND GIBSON'S CAVE    3m (5km)

Maps: OS Sheets Landranger 92; Outdoor Leisure 31.

*A delightful little walk with no difficult sections.*

Start: At 909284, Bowlees Picnic Area.

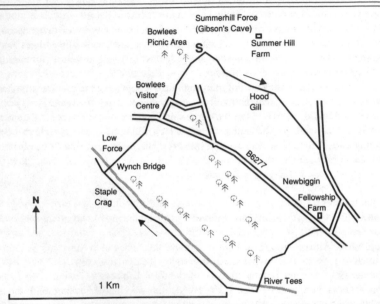

Leave the Picnic Area over a cattle grid, and at a hairpin bend go straight ahead to a gate. From here can be seen the whitewashed houses of Bowlees and, in the middle distance, the Whinstone crags of Holwick Scar. Whinstone is a hard, volcanic rock used for surfacing roads. The way ahead, through gates, is along Hood Gill beyond which a stone bridge, and then a stile, are crossed. The plantations here are larch and pine, with much mature ash and sycamore with a few oak and, some distance away, the junipers of High Force. Trees flourish in this fertile area and provide welcome shelter for livestock. Continue in a south easterly direction to a second stile at a field gate. Cross and go right, along the minor road to Newbiggin. Turn right down a narrow road with Fellowship Farm on one side of it and its farmyard on the other. On reaching a T-junction turn right along the main road for 50 yards to reach a stile on its left-hand side. Cross the field ahead on a clear path to reach a stile. Cross this and then cross

Bowlees Beck. Continue past, on your right, a limestone ridge on which a lot of beech trees have become established, thriving on the limestone. Go through a field gate by an old barn and cross the River Tees by Scoberry Bridge. The walk joins the Pennine Way here: go right along it, following the riverbank upstream. To your left as you cross a wooden stile are some medieval iron mines. Soon a wooden bridge is reached: cross to reach a stile close to Staple Crag, a great Whinstone buttress. It is here that the River Tees narrows into a gorge just below Low Force. **Wynch Bridge** spans the river: cross the bridge and go away from the river along a clear path through woods. Squeeze through a stone stile at the wood edge. Known as 'fat ladies' torment, this stile, both sides of which weigh about 1 ton, was placed there by an anonymous stile builder using only the muscles of man and horse. Cross the meadows ahead to reach a kissing gate on to a road. Cross with car, and continue along the lane to Bowlees. Go through a gate on your right to return to the entrance to the picnic area. Once across Bowlees Beck follow the signs, upstream, to **Gibson's Cave** which is behind Summerhill Force. This path is a permissive path, the permission being from the Raby Estates.

POINTS OF INTEREST:
**Wynch Bridge** – The present Wynch Bridge dates from 1830. An earlier bridge was built in 1704 – possibly the first suspension bridge in Europe – with a handrail on one side only. In 1820, as 11 haymakers were crossing, its main chain snapped and one man was drowned.
**Gibson's Cave** – Gibson was a 16th century outlaw who hid and lived behind Summerhill Force when pursued by the constables of Barnard Castle.
The large building seen en route is Holwick Lodge, the Earl of Strathmore's shooting house where the Queen Mother spent part of her honeymoon. It looks more like Dracula's Castle than a lodge.

Maps: OS Sheets Landranger 92; Pathfinder NZ 12/13.

*A most interesting walk along tracks, passing mining and industrial remains.*

Start: At 100256, the Quarry Lane picnic site.

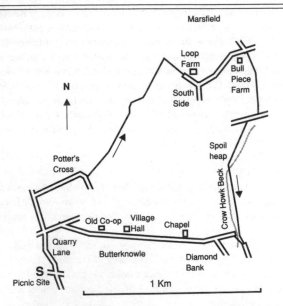

From the picnic area, just beyond the west end of Butterknowle, turn left into Quarry Lane and at the main road go directly across and continue long the wide track ahead. The track forms part of the old burial route to Hamsterley Church some 4 miles to the north. At the first big house fork right along another track, going through two gates in front of a farm to reach a small cluster of attractive cottages at Potters Cross. There, join a narrow road which soon bends to the right: leave it at this point going through a gate on your left and passing in front of some cottages, also on the left. Go through another gate and then straight across the field ahead. Go through a gate and over a stile to cross a stream on a footbridge. Keep ahead to cross another stile in a fence, and continue along the left side of the next two fields to reach a third one. Here, turn right and go along the fence on your right to reach a stile next to a gate. Go over on to a track past Loop Farm which leads to a road at South Side. Turn left along the road for $^1/_4$ mile, passing Bull Piece Farm on your right. Just past the farm, where the road bends, go over a stile in the hedge on your right and continue along the right side of three fields, crossing stiles, to reach another quiet, country road. Now turn right, along the road for about 50 yards and there go left, along a path which goes alongside Crow Howle Beck. This very pleasant path will lead you to an old colliery spoil heap: keep going beyond this, passing, to the right, the remains of the colliery blacksmith's shop. Cross a facing stile, but do not go as far as the bridge ahead. Instead, turn left along the course of the old **Butterknowle to Haggerleases branch railway line.** Continue past industrial remains on your left to reach a large concrete bridge just short of the first houses of Butterknowle. Cross this bridge and climb a path to the houses in Stone Row. Continue ahead, past the village school, and along the main street. At the end of the village, where the road bends right, take the footpath on the left past the front of two houses to reach Quarry Lane. Turn left, back to the picnic area.

POINTS OF INTEREST:
**Butterknowle to Haggerleases branch railway line** – The line was built specifically to serve the Butterknowle and Marsfield Collicry. The railway closed in 1910 along with the whole complex of industrial activity in this small valley.

# Walk 12  BUTTERKNOWLE AND THE RIVER GAUNLESS  3m (5km)
## Maps: OS Sheets Landranger 92; Pathfinder NZ 12/13.
*A pleasant walk along field paths to the River Gaunless.*
Start: At 100256, the Quarry Lane picnic site.

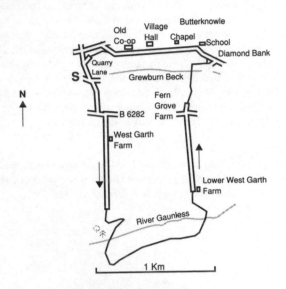

From the picnic site, just beyond the west end of Butterknowle village, turn right into Quarry Lane and go along it to the B6282. Cross, turn left for a few yards and then turn right, opposite a terrace of houses, on to a track. Continue down this for $^1/_2$ mile, passing several farms and buildings. At the end of the track go straight ahead, through a gate, and continue alongside a hedge on your left to another gate in the left corner of the field. Go through this gate and turn left along the top of a bank to reach a stone wall and a pine tree. Turn right and descend to a gate in a stone wall, beyond which the River Gaunless flows. Go through the gate and cross the river on stones. Bear right, up the opposite bank, through bracken, to the right corner of a facing wall. At this point there is a wooded gill on your right.

Continue ahead, close to a wall on your left, and aim for a bridge over the old Bishop Auckland to Barnard Castle railway line. Do not cross it. Instead, go down the embankment to the left on to the trackbed, and go left along it. The view from the line over the Gaunless Valley towards Butterknowle and beyond is very good. Where the track bends to the right, towards a farm, continue ahead for a short distance. Now, before crossing a bridge, drop down the embankment on the left and go towards a footbridge over the River Gaunless at the bottom of the slope. Cross the footbridge and bear left through a field and up a bank to a gate at the top. Go through this and continue forward, close to a wall on the left, to a track in front of a barn. Turn right along the track, past the barn, then left, along a concrete drive, going in front of Lower West Garth Farm. Follow the drive for $\frac{1}{2}$ mile to the B6282. Cross the road and go down the drive of Fern Grove Farm, immediately opposite. Keeping to the right of the farmhouse, go through a gate and then over a stile in a wooden fence. Cross the left side of the next field and go down steps to cross Grewburn Beck. Immediately turn right over a stile, and go along a path up **Diamond Bank** and through the remains of Old Diamond Colliery to reach a kissing gate. Go through and turn sharp left to reach another gate on to a road at Diamond Bank. Turn left up the hill, and continue through the main street of Butterknowle, passing the Wesleyan Chapel on your right and, 100 yards beyond it and on the left, a workshop and a warehouse. A little further along, on your right, is the old Co-operative Store. At the end of the village, where the road bends right, take the footpath on the left, past the front of two houses, to reach Quarry Lane. Turn left into the picnic area where the walk began.

POINTS OF INTEREST:
**Diamond Bank** – A stone slab in the wall behind the pavement, marked with an arrow, marks the spot where a local policeman, Sergeant Smith, was murdered in 1884.
The second house on the right down the track leading south from the B6282 is where Brian Fletcher, the jockey, lived. He rode three Grand National winners, including Red Rum.

REFRESHMENTS:
Sorry, none!

# Walk 13    HAMSTERLEY FOREST AND CROSSFIELD    3m (5km)

Maps: OS Sheets Landranger 92; Outdoor Leisure 31.

*A splendid little forest walk in one of the region's major attractions.*

Start: The Information Centre, Hamsterley Forest.

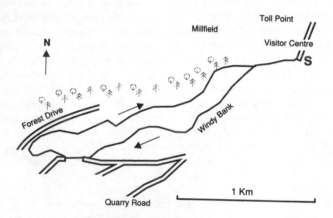

In order to more fully appreciate what this interesting and informative walk has to offer, a visit to the Centre's exhibition is strongly advised.

Walk westwards along the Forest Drive for a little way and follow a track on the left which soon bridges Bedburn Beck. On this section of the walk the trees are a pleasing mix of broad-leaved deciduous species – alder, ash, silver birch and willow, while from the bridge over Bedburn Beck dippers are frequently seen. Once over the bridge, pass a bird cherry on your right and take the path to Windy Bank Wood, uphill and to the right. Here the woodland is a rich blend with many conifers – Sitka spruce, Scots pine, Western hemlock, European larch, Japanese larch, Norway spruce, Douglas fir and Grand fir. Red squirrels are also still found here. This part of the forest – called Crossfield Plantation – supports a wide variety of trees because the soil on the hillside is very fertile: so great is the canopy of foliage that little undergrowth has a chance to develop, though on the pathsides several species such as coltsfoot, March thistle and foxglove are evident. The area is very attractive to Roe deer, which are mostly likely to be seen on summer evenings or winter mornings: their tracks, or 'slots', are frequently seen.

Passing over the brow of the hill the path descends to meet a metalled road at a tangent. Continue along this for a little way, then take a path, to the right, back to Bedburn Beck, passing **Hamsterley Forest**'s only plantation of very tall Grand Fir. Cross Bedburn Beck on a bridge and go right, along a forest drive for just over $^1/_2$ mile. On approaching Low Redford, turn right off the forest drive along a path that leads down to the confluence of Bedburn and Ayhope Becks. Cross Ayhope Beck on a bridge and take the path beside Bedburn Beck back to the start.

POINTS OF INTEREST:
**Hamsterley Forest** – Although a commercially productive forest of 2,000 hectares (5,000 acres) the Forest, which is managed by the Forestry Commission, offers several facilities for recreation including information displays, waymarked walks, a forest drive, literature, car parks, picnic areas and toilets.

REFRESHMENTS:
None, please bring your own to eat in the picnic areas.

# Walk 14    SALTER'S GATE AND TUNSTALL RESERVOIR    3¹/₄m (5.2km)

Maps: OS Sheets Landranger 87 & 88; Pathfinder NZ 04/14.

*A walk especially suited to nature-lovers.*

Start: At 077426, Salter's Gate.

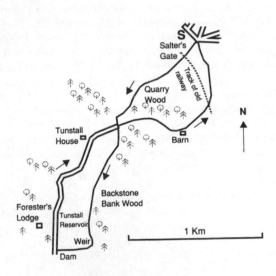

From the road junctions at Salter's Gate cross a white stile and continue along a path over a field, exiting at a stile. Cross a **dis-used railway line** to a wicket gate from where there are excellent views of the Tunstall Valley and the surrounding moors. Continue across through pasture to go through a facing gate. Keeping close to **Quarry Wood** on your left, descend to **Tunstall Reservoir** – now in full view ahead. At the foot of the hill go through a gate just past a sign warning people of danger from adders. Cross a stile on your left and take the pleasant shoreline path: it is not a public right of way but as long as visitors observe the byelaws the Water Authority welcomes them. On your left as you walk along the eastern side of Tunstall Reservoir is Blackstone Bank Wood, one of the few surviving natural oak woods in West Durham. Most of the other woodland around the reservoir was first planted with pine, spruce and larch, during

36

the last 100 years. On reaching a track that leads to the dam, turn right along it, crossing the dam and turning right at its western end on to a road. The dam is an ideal place from which to observe geese and duck wintering on the reservoir. The Victorian Mansion on your left is Forester's Lodge, rebuilt after the reservoir drowned the original house. Continue northwards along the road, edging the reservoir, and after $^1/_2$ mile a picnic area, with parking and toilets, is reached. Here a bridge carries a road over a feeder. To the left of it there is a fine bird cherry tree. Continue towards the head of the reservoir and Tunstall House, an 18th century dales farm. When a farm track is reached, go right along it and cross the bridge. The head of the reservoir to your left is reserved for wild life. Once back on the eastern bank go straight ahead for a 400 feet climb back to Salter's Gate, first going through Quarry Wood, then continuing along its edge, to the left. About $^1/_4$ mile after leaving the wood the dis-used railway line is rejoined near some depot buildings. Go left, along the track-bed briefly, then bear right, through a gate and go northwards along a clear track. Go through a gate midway along it and return to the same white stile crossed on the outward journey.

POINTS OF INTEREST:

**Dis-used railway line** – The line was built by the Stockton and Darlington Railway Company in 1845 to link the New Derwent Iron Company's works at Consett with Crook.

**Tunstall Reservoir** – Constructed in 1879 to supply drinking water to Willington, Shildon, Sedgefield and Spennymoor. When the valley was flooded three houses and many acres of farm and woodland were drowned.

**Quarry Wood** – The haunt of foxes and roe deer. There is still evidence of quarrying but old spoil heaps were planted with larch trees 60 – 70 years ago, an early example of land reclamation.

# Walk 15   AUCKLAND CASTLE PARK AND VINOVIA   3¹/₂m (5.5km)

Maps: OS Sheets Landranger 93; Pathfinder NZ 23/33.

*An easy walk best done when the Castle and Fort are open.*

Start: Bishop Auckland clock tower.

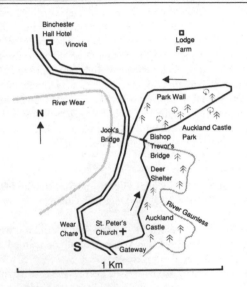

From the clock tower, which separates the castle from the market place, go along a formal pathway and turn left into **Auckland Castle Park**. The depressions halfway down the slope, seen from the corner of the castle wall, were medieval fish ponds. Waste food from the kitchens was recycled through these ponds, being fed to carp which were caught and served at the Bishop's table. Bear right to the shelter from where deer used to be fed in winter to ensure they remained worth hunting. Continue along a ridge path that leads down to Bishop Trevor's Bridge, and continue straight ahead along the path, passing a building once used for storing ice underground. The golf course seen across Coundon Burn was once part of the hunting park. On reaching the top of a hill a Wellingtonia is passed. This species of tree has a spongy bark and for this reason was said to have been used as a punch bag by prize fighters. The route leaves the inner, walled, park and goes sharp left along the wall. The stone copings on your left were rounded to keep water out of the wall.

Follow the path around the park wall to the Newfield Road and turn right near Jack's Bridge which carries the road and the wall over the River Gaunless, a stream which has its source near Egglestone in Teesdale. On reaching Binchester Hall turn right up the hotel drive where the retaining wall on your right appears to contain stones from Vinovia, the Roman name for Binchester. The name means 'pleasant spot'. Part of the fort has recently been excavated and is open to the public from early April to the end of September – daily, except Tuesdays and Wednesdays. Return to the road and retrace your steps towards Bishop Auckland. On the opposite bank of the River Wear, on your right, a flood bank protects a large area of productive land from the river when it is in spate. On this section of the walk there are good views of St Peter's Chapel over the wall on your left. Turn left up steep and narrow Wear Chare, and continue anti-clockwise round the Town Hall back to the start of the walk.

## POINTS OF INTEREST:
**Auckland Castle Park** – Bishop Hatfield, like other Bishops of Durham, had the job of keeping the Scots at bay. In 1346, while he was in France, laying siege to Calais, the king of Scotland marched south with a large army sacking Hexham and heading for Durham. An English army of 16,000 men with horses, baggage train and tents camped in Auckland Castle Park on the night of October, 16th 1346. The next day they marched nine miles to encounter the Scots at the Battle of Neville's Cross, which they won.

A Roman road, Dere Street, linked the forts in Durham at Piercebridge, Lanchester, Ebchester and Binchester. It is believed to run where Auckland Castle now stands.

## REFRESHMENTS:
Hotels, pubs and cafés in Bishop Auckland.

# Walk 16    LITTLETOWN AND PITTINGTON HILL    3½m (5.5km)
## Maps: OS Sheets Landranger 88; Pathfinder NZ 24/34.
*One steep climb up Pittington Hill, but otherwise an easy walk.*
Start: The Duke of York, Littletown.

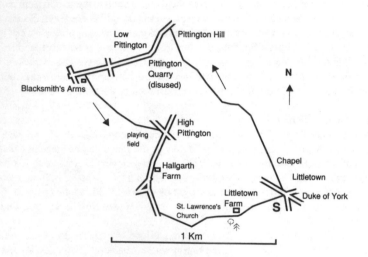

From The Duke of York take the path to the left of some cottages near the old chapel. Where the path joins a track go right, alongside a concrete gully which carries water from the reclaimed colliery heaps. Cross a bridge and go uphill. Cross a minor road and climb the steep path up Pittington Hill. The slope is steep and rocky, making it difficult for the trees to stay upright: with little top soil the roots must penetrate the limestone for support. On reaching the top of the hill the all round views are excellent and the expected windswept moorland turns out to be green fields, a most pleasing surprise. Continue along the path around the field ahead and partly down the far side of the hill where it weaves among old hawthorn trees, which give shade and shelter to the livestock. On reaching a facing path go left along it, crossing a stile and edging a wood on your left, to a kissing gate. Go through on to a road leading southwards from the disused Pittington Quarry on your left. Follow the road, passing the hamlet of

Low Pittington, which like so many hamlets on the coalfield did not have any colliery terraces attached to it: the Durham farming community remained separate from the mining village. Cross the road at Green Acres Stud and, in less than $^1/_4$ mile, go left, eastwards, through two gates to a path along a former railway. Follow this into a cutting. On reaching **High Pittington** go right along Hall Lane to Hallgarth Farm. Continue along the path curving left past **St Lawrence's Church**. Cross a bridge over a stream. Ignoring sideroads going first right, then left, go straight ahead past Littletown Farm. Cross the field ahead aiming for a hedge on the left and guided by the curbs of an ancient track which leads back to the Duke of York.

POINTS OF INTEREST:
**High Pittington** – Sheltered by a grove of elm and sycamore, the village was once the country retreat of the Prior of the Abbey of Durham.
**St Lawrence's Church** – Contains a Norman font which was once sold for half a crown ($12^1/_2$p) and used as a feeding trough at Belmont Farm. In 1885 it was re-discovered, after 76 years.

REFRESHMENTS:
*The Duke of York*, Littletown (tel no: 091 372 0440).
*The Blacksmith's Arms*, Green Acres Stud (tel no: 091 372 0287).

# Walk 17     SHINCLIFFE WOOD     3½m (5.5km)

Maps: OS Sheets Landranger 88 & 93; Pathfinder NZ 23/33 & NZ 24/34.

*An easy walk which may be slippery near High Butterby when it is wet.*

Start: Shincliffe Post Office.

From the Post Office turn left into 'Heathways' to cut through a modern housing estate. Turn left again on approaching 'Hillcrest'. From here there is a fine view of Durham Cathedral. Descend to the bottom of the hill to where two houses, once the original church school, overlook a layby. Cross the main road at the Seven Stars and follow the road past the cemetery wall to the church path. Turn left along the path. The church was built in 1850 for £1,600. Go between the Rectory and the Church Hall to reach the middle of Shincliffe, a village noted for its prettiness and its masses of spring flowers. There turn right, then left past a garden centre. Continue southwards, passing – on the far side of the river on your right – an Agricultural College. A little further on, closer to the path, **Shincliffe Hall** is passed. It once housed landgirls but is

42

now University accommodation. Stay with the path, first edging, then going through Shincliffe Wood which is managed by the Dean and Chapter of Durham Cathedral. The land beside the river here is protected by manmade flood banks, some built by 14th century monks.

The path edges the river on the outside of a bend: there is a danger of erosion so care is needed. On leaving the wood the path climbs steeply to High Butterby Farm, beyond which, in a small field on your right, there is a good example of the long abandoned farming practice of ridge and furrow. At a crossing of paths turn left, northwards, along Strawberry Lane which was probably used by Roman legions and was certainly used by peasants and yeoman farmers driving cattle between Ferryhill and Durham City. Follow the lane past the grandstand of **Shincliffe Racecourse**, which is now used for storing hay. Soon, to the right, High Grange Farm is passed. The narrowness of the main building shows the age of this pantile-roofed house: early builders had difficulty roofing wide buildings. The derelict building on the left is where explosives were stored for Bowburn Colliery. Soon the track becomes a tarmac road leading to the A177. Cross the road to return to the start of the walk.

POINTS OF INTEREST:
**Shincliffe Hall** – The hall was built of local materials – handmade bricks and a stone slab roof – for a Georgian gentleman. Slates were not used in Durham until Victorian times.
**Shincliffe Racecourse** – Opened in 1913 to replace Durham City Racecourse which had become University playing fields. The venture failed because of the 1914-18 war.

REFRESHMENTS:
*The Seven Stars*, Shincliffe (tel no: 091 3848454).

# Walk 18   HAMSTERLEY AND THE POSTMAN'S ROUTE   3½m (5.5km)

Maps: OS Sheets Landranger 92; Outdoor Leisure 31.

*Mainly along forest roads and paths. Waymarked at first with purple arrows, then with blue ones.*

Start: At 067299, The Grove, Hamsterley Forest.

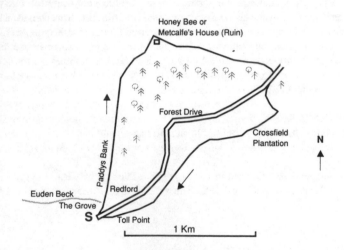

Leave the Grove along a track that used to be an old coach road to Wolsingham, and cross Euden Beck on a footbridge at Red Ford. Continue along a track up Paddy's Bank to the hilltop from where the views of the surrounding forest are good. Now go along an old road down to the remains of Honey Bee House – sometimes referred to as Metcalfe's House – following purple arrows. From the House the walk takes a forest drive along the valley of the Ayhope Beck. On the more open areas of this path, where the young trees are growing, many species of butterfly can be seen. Slow worms, common lizards and adders can also be found, especially on warm spring and summer days. Adders are Britain's only poisonous snakes and are the only snakes common in County Durham: they are harmless if left alone. Continue walking uphill along the

44

road as it curves to the left, passing oaks, western hemlock, European and Japanese larch and Scots pine. After passing the highest point the road descends a hillside that has recently been felled and replanted. The view across the valley from here is of pasture, moor and both coniferous and broad-leafed woodland. Where the walk leaves the forest road through a gate look out for red squirrels, this is one of the best places in the forest from which to see them.

On reaching the forest road, cross it and follow the blue arrows of the Postman's Route, so named because part of it was used by local postmen delivering mail in the forest. Cross Ayhope Beck and continue through Crossfield Plantation, going up the hill and to the right, through conifers, to reach the Grove Bridge which spans Spurtswood Beck. The bridge was built by the Surtees family who owned nearby Grove House and the estate which is now Hamsterley Forest. It stands on the site of the ford it replaced. On the upstream side of the bridge there is a coat of arms. Cross the bridge and, shortly after, reach the picnic area where the walk began.

POINTS OF INTEREST:
Shy roe deer may be seen along the route, particularly on summer evenings or winter mornings. Their footprints, which are usually smaller and more pointed than those of sheep, are called 'slots'.

**BOWES AND THE RIGG**           3¹/₂m (5.5km)

Maps: OS Sheets Landranger 92; Outdoor Leisure 30.

*An excellent walk along quiet lanes and tracks, and across moorland.*

Start: The car park, Bowes.

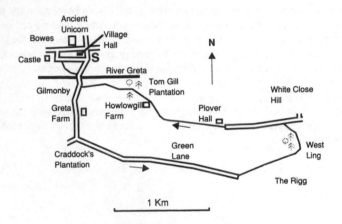

From the car park near the crossroads at the eastern end of Bowes go up the village, passing the Ancient Unicorn Hotel on your right. At the top of the hill turn left down a narrow lane beside St Cuthbert's church. Continue along the lane, which soon turns left, away from the castle. A little way beyond the left turn go over a stile next to a gate on your right. Go diagonally left across two fields to enter woods above the River Greta. Follow a path down a bank to meet a road close to Gilmonby Bridge. Turn right, along the road, passing buildings and the road end to Gilmonby on your right, and continue ahead, passing Greta Farm on your left. Where the road bifurcates, take the left fork from which there are extensive, all-round views which include Stang Forest, on your distant right. After about 1 mile, where the tarmac road ends, go ahead through a gate and along a walled green lane to a gate at its far end. Go through to The Rigg, which is part of Scargill Low Moor.

Bear left, through long grass and heather and aim towards the right side of a distant plantation. Just past the plantation there are a stone building and the ruined West Ling farmhouse to the left: go between them and through a gate next to the building. Go ahead to a stile in a facing wall. Go through and diagonally left across a field to reach a track from **White Close Hill Farm**. Go left, along it, to Plover Hall Farm.

Keep to the left of the farm buildings and follow their walls, leaving the track, to reach a corner stile into a wooded enclosure. Go ahead over four fields to join the drive to Howlowgill Farm, briefly. Continue through the field to the right of the buildings, taking care when crossing any electric wire fences which may have been erected. Go diagonally left and downhill to a track which crosses a gill and, once across it, bear right over another field to a stile leading into Tom Gill Plantation, seen ahead. Cross the stile and take a path through the plantation, crossing a small bridge and leaving the trees over a stile into a large field. Cross this field, aiming for the plantation corner ahead and slightly to your right. Continue over three more fields, going over two stiles to reach the road used earlier through a kissing gate. Turn right over Gilmonby Bridge, soon reaching the car park.

POINTS OF INTEREST:
**White Close Hill Farm** – From the walk section near the farm the views ahead include Bowes, the castle and, beyond, the summit of Mickle Fell which at 2,591 feet (790 metres) is the highest point in County Durham.

REFRESHMENTS:
*The Ancient Unicorn Hotel*, Bowes (tel no: 0833 28321).

Walk 20          **BEAMISH WOODS**          4m (6.5km)

Maps: OS Sheets Landranger 88; Pathfinder NZ 05/15 & NZ 25/35.

*An ideal walk from which to see industrial archaeology in pleasant country surroundings.*

Start: At 205551, Beamishburn Picnic Area.

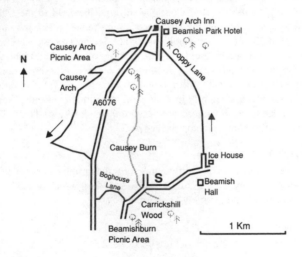

From the Picnic Area go right, along the road towards **Beamish Hall**. Turn left along Coppy Lane, an unsurfaced track, but before doing so a small detour of a few yards along the surfaced road will bring you to an old ice house built into the wall on your left. In this, ice from the fish ponds was stored for use at a later date. Go along Coppy Lane, passing between fields and woods, to reach, after 1 mile, the surfaced Beamishburn road near Causey Arch Inn. Part of the lane was once a wagon-way along which coal was carried. The coal provided the wealth that maintained the lifestyle of the Hall owners.

Turn left along Beamishburn road. Go right at a stile and cross fields along a stiled public footpath to reach the A6076, a road built to create employment during the depression of the 1930's. Cross the road and continue along a clear path to the Causey Arch Picnic Area, which contains both **Causey Arch** and some huge embankments and a culvert built in 1725. Go down to the stream and approach the Arch from below to see it at its best. Climb the steps to the Arch, cross it, and go right, along the former track of the Tanfield Railway towards Stanley.

After about $^3/_4$ mile turn left up a flight of steps and cross a field on a stiled path to reach the A6076. Turn right, along it, to reach Bog House Lane on your left. This lane once formed the boundary between the Shaftoe and the Clavering Estates and linked Beamish Mill with Tanfield long before Stanley existed. Go left, along the lane, crossing four stiles to reach the Beamishburn road. Cross and enter Carricks Hill Wood through a doorway in a wall. Go through the wood on a clear path. Leave the path to cross Beamish Burn by a bridge to return to the picnic area.

## POINTS OF INTEREST:

**Beamish Hall** – The Lords of Beamish were, from the time of the Norman Conquest, also the Lords of Tanfield and Kibblesworth. The first record of a grand house on the estate is in 1309 when Bertram Mon Goucher acquired a wife who brought the Beamish Estate as a dowry. The house and grounds have subsequently been occupied by the Percys, Edens and Shaftoes.

**Causey Arch** – Even by today's standards the Causey Arch works are substantial. For them to have been built before the steam engine had been invented with muscle power as the only means of mobile energy called for prodigious feats of engineering.

## REFRESHMENTS:

*The Beamish Park Hotel*, (tel no: 0207 230666).

# Walk 21  BARNARD CASTLE AND FLATTS WOOD    4m (6.5km)
Maps: OS Sheets Landranger 92; Outdoor Leisure 31.

*A silvan walk along the east bank of the River Tees. Waymarked throughout.*

Start: The Tourist Information Centre, Galgate, Barnard Castle.

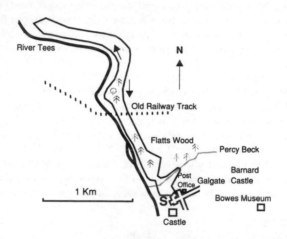

From the Information Centre go left, down Galgate, to the Three Horseshoes pub. Cross Galgate, using a zebra crossing, towards the Post Office, and cross Flatts Road next to it. Continue alongside the Methodist Chapel for about 40 yards to reach an information board. From here take the wide tarmac path on your right, going between children's swings and a paddling pool, and continue along a descending path to reach the River Tees in Flatts Wood. Ignoring the aqueduct bridge on your left, continue along the path, briefly, to cross a wooden footbridge over Percy Beck, a Tees feeder. Continue upstream along the riverbank, following a waymarked route and ignoring all paths on your right. Should you wish to shorten the walk, take one of these paths up the wooded bank to reach the path used for the return journey at its top. These branching paths are **not** public rights of way: they are 'permissive' paths.

Keep following the main path upstream, going below the buttress of the Tees Valley viaduct, which once carried the railway line from Barnard Castle to Kirkby Stephen, and descending into an area of tall pines to climb and drop again to the water's edge. This part of the route, called the Rock Walk, passes between two boulders called 'wishing stones' and climbs a stone staircase between some overhanging yew trees. After $^1/_2$ mile ignore the path on your right, and continue ahead to reach a gate in a facing wall. Go through and along the right-hand side of the field ahead. After 100 yards go through a gate in a facing wall. Climb the steep slope ahead to a fence. Cross, and go right along it. The walk now follows the edge of several fields, going through gates, to where the path goes to the right of a stone wall, and then a fence along the edge of a wood. When an old railway track is reached, go right for a few yards, then left, to continue along the wood's edge. Keep along the fence edging the wood to reach a 'permissive' path where the fence bends sharply. The path also bends, left, and descends to another path along Percy Beck. Here turn left, briefly, then right over a footbridge, and climb steps to reach the end of Raby Avenue. Go along this to reach Galgate, close to the Post Office near where the walk began.

## POINTS OF INTEREST:
En route to the viaduct buttress, the path passes part of Flatts Wood that has been felled by Raby Estates for timber and to remove trees stricken by Dutch Elm disease. With more light now reaching the ground a new habitat has been created for birds, plants and animals that contrasts nicely with the denser wooded areas, thereby adding interest.

## REFRESHMENTS:
Hotels, pubs and cafés in Barnard Castle.

Walk 22  **MIDDLETON-IN-TEESDALE AND SNAISGILL**  4m (6.5km)

Maps: OS Sheets Landranger 92; Outdoor Leisure 31.

*A fascinating blend of woodland scenery and field walking, with glorious views of Upper Teesdale.*

Start: Middleton-in-Teesdale Car Park.

From the car park go left, past the memorial fountain, along Market Place. Pass the church on your right, and go uphill along the Stanhope road. On reaching unsurfaced Beck Road, which leads into woodland, go left along it, descending to Hudeshope Beck. Continue upstream along a beckside path, passing the pleasant Horse Shoe Falls to return to Beck Road. Just before it divides, prior to crossing the beck, go right along a rough track, edging fir trees on your right. Cross a band of rubble and go right, as directed by a yellow arrow on a facing tree stump. Follow a narrow path, edging the wood on your right, climbing steadily. Turn sharp left along the edge of Snaisgill, passing a yellow marker which directs you to a signposted stile in the top left-hand corner of the wood. Cross the stile on to a minor road and go right. The road goes through Snaisgill, curving right and passing, on the left, first a roadside house, then one set back in its own grounds. Beyond the second house there is a signposted stile: cross and continue over the field ahead to a stile in its right corner, near a telegraph post. Cross the next field diagonally right over a new stile 25 yards along the wall on our right.

Continue diagonally left to a right-hand corner stile which has both a little gate and a yellow arrow. Cross the next field as directed by this arrow to another stile. Cross the next field diagonally left to a facing wall where, 25 yards short of the right-hand corner, you cross a stile. Go diagonally right across the next field towards its top right-hand corner and over the next field diagonally right to a wall stile to the right of a field house. Cross the next field diagonally right to a stile at a footpath sign, leading to a minor road. Cross to another signposted stile. Descend the field ahead, close to a wall on your left, and cross a stile in the corner of a facing wall. Continue down the next field, ignoring a stile on your left, and on approaching a facing wall, beyond which is Stanhope Gate Farm, turn right along a cart track to a gate. Go through and past the right side of the farm buildings, going under an underpass, between a wall and a row of trees, and into a very short lane. At a facing wall, go right over a stile into a field. Cross to a stile in a facing wall. Go diagonally right to a gate a third of the way down the field, beyond crossing an adjoining stile into the next one. Leave a farm track and go diagonally left to a stile adjoining another gate a third of the way down this field. Cross the corner of the next field, diagonally left to a little gate. Go through and continue diagonally right down the next field to a stile to the left of some electricity poles. Turn left in the next field, crossing it close to a wall on your left, to reach a revolving gate in a fence. Go through on to a little lane. Turn right and take the first turning left into Middleton's main street. Cross diagonally right to reach the car park.

REFRESHMENTS:
Hotels, pubs and cafés in Middleton-in-Teesdale.

# Walk 23 THE KING'S WALK 4m (6.5km)

Maps: OS Sheets Landranger 92; Outdoor Leisure 31.

*A lovely, waymarked walk through woodland and fields.*

Start: The Memorial Fountain, Middleton-in-Teesdale.

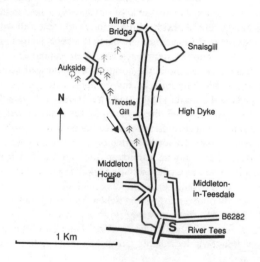

From the fountain cross the road, go past the war memorial and along Wesley Terrace. At the end, take the footpath uphill past a beech hedge hiding a churchyard. Stay on the path as it turns left then right into a field. Within a few yards go over a stile on your left into a courtyard and continue diagonally right up two steps and along a narrow passage to a road. Turn right for about 60 yards, then go left along another road into woods. Almost immediately go right, through trees on a rough track. This track is called King's Walk and is not a public right of way: Raby Estates have granted permission for people to walk along it. The track climbs through pine and beech trees and curves right up a short, steep hill to a barn on the right. Bear left with the track as it continues upwards, through trees, and descends to cross Snaisgill Beck over a wooden bridge. Continue left, along a narrow path, to a stone wall on the edge of the plantation. Turn left along the edge of the trees, descending to a track by some disused lime kilns.

Turn left, briefly, on to Beck road and turn right along it, crossing Hudeshope Beck on Miner's Bridge. Go through a field gate immediately on the left, and go along the riverbank. Cross a feeder and aim for a facing fence. On reaching it, do not cross the stile. Instead go right, uphill, along the fence on your left, and at the hilltop turn right and follow a stone wall for a short distance to a stile on your left. Cross into a larger field. Go diagonally left across it, climbing gently, past a small pond to a stile. Cross and follow the left wall to another stile in its left corner, near a barn. Cross and go left, downhill, along a minor road for about 250 yards. Turn left through the gates next to a large house called 'Aukside Villa' into a large field. Keep to the right side for a further 250 yards to cross a small, stone slab bridge. Go over a wall stile and continue in the same direction across two fields, passing a small barn on your left, to reach a small wooden gate in the field's corner. Go through and along a narrow path beside Throstle Gill with a stone wall on your right. Descend gradually to join a wider track in the woods and turn right along it, before going left in front of a house. Go down steps between cottages, and turn right along the road for a short distance to a small gap in the wall opposite. Follow the path alongside the parkland in front of Middleton House and Clock Tower to join another road. Cross with care. Turn left past the old lead company school, then right down a track to a footbridge over Hudeshope Beck. Continue along the path to Bridge Street and turn left along to the fountain.

POINTS OF INTEREST:
Limestone from the nearby Skeers Quarry was burnt in the kilns near Beck Road and the lime used to improve the local soil.

REFRESHMENTS:
Hotels, pubs and cafés in Middleton-in-Teesdale.

# Walk 24    **BOWLEES AND HIGH FORCE**    4m (6.5km)

Maps: OS Sheets Landranger 92; Outdoor Leisure 31.

*An excellent walk to High Force, England's largest waterfall.*

Start: The Bowlees Picnic Area car park.

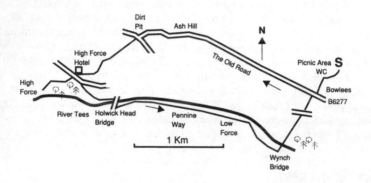

From the car park cross Bowlees Beck, pass the visitor centre and go on to a minor road. Turn right through a gate to reach the old Teesdale road which was used to carry traffic along the dale before the London Lead Company built what is now the B6277 along the valley bottom, around 1840. Follow the track uphill, going through several gates and passing Ash Hill Farm and a lonesome pine on your left. From here the views up and down Teesdale are lovely and in the distance below can be seen the wooded gorge leading to High Force. Continue downhill to the tiny hamlet of Dirt Pit, a name derived from 'deerpath', and keep going to a minor road. Cross to reach a field over a wooden stile. Cross this large field, going through a boggy area in the middle of it, then bearing left, uphill, to a gateway. Go through, continue past a small barn and head for the top left corner of the field. Go through another gate and immediately turn left over a stile.

Descend to go through the picnic area and car park adjoining the High Force Hotel, to reach the B6277. Across the road is the entrance to the wooded gorge and **High Force** waterfall. A small charge is made at the entrance kiosk, but the walk through the gorge to the fall is most impressive and the fall itself is majestic, especially after a period of heavy rainfall. Returning to the entrance kiosk go right, along the road, for several yards and take the steep path on your right through trees, using stone steps which bring you to a gate. Beyond, the Tees is reached. Go left, along the riverbank, to Holwick Head Bridge where the river is crossed. Now turn left along the river's south bank for about 1 mile to reach Low Force falls, below which re-cross the Tees on the Wynch Bridge, which dates from 1830. Follow the path between trees, exiting by way of a narrow stone stile, and go across two fields to reach the B6277. Cross and go up a minor road opposite, soon passing the Bowlees Visitor Centre and returning to the picnic area.

POINTS OF INTEREST:
**High Force** – This dramatic falls has been formed over thousands of years by the wearing away of layers of shale and limestone from between sections of hard volcanic whinstone. The slow cutting back of the waterfall is still continuing, gradually extending the length of the gorge, but since the building of Cow Green reservoir upstream, the water coming over the falls is more controlled.

REFRESHMENTS:
*High Force Hotel*, Higher Teesdale (tel no: 0833 22264).

# Walk 25     STAINDROP AND SCAIFE HOUSE     4m (6.5km)

Maps: OS Sheets Landranger 92; Pathfinder NZ 12/13.

*An excellent walk through lush lower Teesdale countryside.*

Start: Staindrop Post Office.

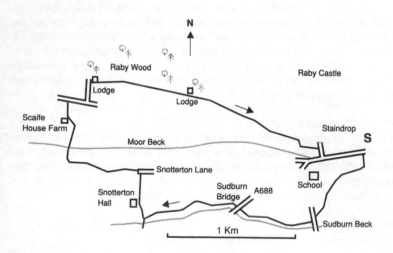

From the post office cross the road and the green and go down the narrow lane to Scarth Hall. At the bottom of the lane turn right to a stile and then bear left across the large field ahead. Go through a gate, across a stone bridge and continue ahead, bearing slightly right to a stile in the hedge opposite. Cross and go towards a double telegraph pole, and on to a stile in a stone wall. Cross to reach a minor road, which is crossed to another stile, beyond which continue alongside Sudburn Beck, going through nine small, narrow fields. After about ¹/₂ mile, climb some steps to reach the main A688 road at Sudburn Bridge. Cross with care, and go over the old road to a stone stile. Cross and go straight ahead to cross a wooden stile. Keep close to Sudburn Beck as it bends left. Soon a gate in a stone wall is reached just below the white painted buildings of Snotterton Hall on your right. Go though the gate and, immediately, a footbridge over Sudburn Beck is reached. Do not cross: instead, climb the field on your right and go through a gate into the farmyard of Snotterton Hall. Keeping to the right of the buildings continue along the farm road from where the views, especially across the lower lying land ahead and to the east, are particularly lovely. **Staindrop Church** is seen in the distance. Where the farm road turns sharp right, go left through a white gate and follow a track along the field edge to a gate into another field. Go through the gate and bear slightly right over the field towards a hedge on your near right which joins the facing boundary at right angles. Continue close to it for about 100 yards, then turn right through a gate and descend a slope to cross Moor Beck. Climb the field towards Scaife House Farm. Go through the farmyard and along a drive to the B6279, the Moor Road. Turn right for $^1/_3$ mile, then go left along a farm track to West Lodge at an entrance to Raby Wood. Just before reaching the lodge turn right, through a gate, and continue alongside a high stone wall on your left to reach a second lodge. There, cross a wooden stile in front of a vegetable garden and, keeping close to the wall, cross two fields using stiles. In the third field stay close to the wall for about $^1/_3$ mile, then go diagonally right to a large stone stile in the field corner. Cross it and continue close to the right side of the next field. Go into the next field, and soon go through a small gap in the hedge on your right. Now follow the narrow path called 'knicky nack' to exit at the corner of North Green in the village. Go through Staindrop to the post office.

POINTS OF INTEREST:
**Staindrop Church** – The church of St Mary is of Saxon origin and was enlarged over the centuries which followed. The tower was heightened in the 15th century. Inside there are some interesting effigies and a fine font constructed from Teesdale marble. The church is the burial place of many members of the Neville family who held Raby Castle for many years.

REFRESHMENTS:
*The Wheatsheaf Inn*, Staindrop (tel no: 0833 60280).

Maps: OS Sheets Landranger 93; Pathfinder NZ 23/33 & 22/32.
*A good, all seasons ramble.*
Start: The Whitworth Road Car Park, Spennymoor.
Finish: The South Church Car Park, Bishop Auckland.

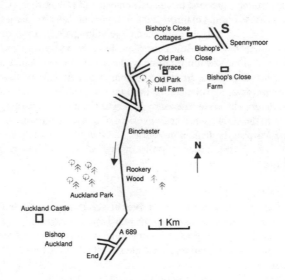

From the Whitworth Road Car Park go westwards, along the **disused line**, through countryside which was once part of the Bishop's Park, passing Bishop's Close Farm and Bishop's Close. Immediately after passing Bishop's Close Cottages the old railway cutting on your left has become a wetland area, and varied bird life and amphibious creatures have been encouraged to make their homes there. After passing Old Park Terrace cottages on your left, go left at a junction and continue across the road to Byers Green Station. The name 'Byers' means 'ancient woods': at one time the village was surrounded by them. The station is now a picnic area with fine views across the Wear Valley. The remains of the station platform are passed before the track goes under a road bridge, now heading in a southerly direction. Soon Binchester is passed. The original Binchester was a Roman military station on Dere Street, to the east of the present Binchester. It was called Vinovia, which means 'pleasant place'.

Beyond Binchester, which is shown on most maps as Binchester Blocks, the route is along a tree-lined embankment which provides excellent cover for many kinds of wildlife and plants. Since the line closed, reclamation, tree planting and Nature herself have created a pleasant route from where the views across the surrounding countryside are good. Beyond the embankment the way is through a cutting. Midway along it a footpath leads away from the line to Vinovia, one mile distant. Continue under a second bridge, which has a story to tell.

When the line was being planned, Bishop Lightfoot insisted that if the line went through his park he should be able to see across it without it obstructing his view. So trees were planted around the bridge and the railway was built into the deep cutting below. Moving from the cutting to an embankment, Auckland Park can be clearly seen on the right: it was once the Bishop's deer park. The golf course, also on the right, is within the walls of the Bishop's Park.

Old Station House is soon reached: it was once Coundon Station. The walk ends at South Church Car Park, where the existing hawthorns and beeches have been complemented with newly planted trees.

POINTS OF INTEREST:

**Disused line** – The line ran from Spennymoor to Bishop Auckland. It was built in 2 stages: in 1841 the section between Byers Green and Spennymoor was opened as part of the Clarence Railway Company's Byers Green Railway, which served Port Clarence on Teesside. This was used to carry coal from the Byers Green and Willington area. Then in 1885 the N E R opened the line between Byers Green and Bishop Auckland the whole line was used by passengers. The complete line formed a link between Bishop Auckland and Cornforth, connecting the Darlington to Bishop Auckland line with the main East Coast route. The line was closed in 1939.

REFRESHMENTS:

Hotels, pubs and cafés at Bishop Auckland and Spennymoor.

# Walk 27    STAINDROP AND CLEATLAM    4m (6.5km)

Maps: OS Sheets Landranger 92; Pathfinder NZ 12/13.

*Wonderful field walking with Cleatlam, a working village, delightfully sited in the middle.*

Start: Staindrop Post Office.

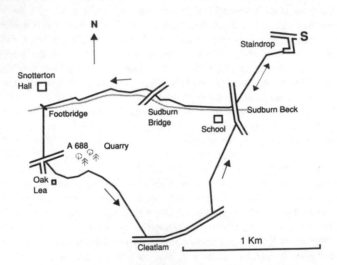

From the Post Office cross the road and the green and go down the narrow lane next to Scarth Hall. At the bottom, turn right to a stile and then bear left across the large field ahead. Go through a gate, cross a stone bridge and bear slightly right to reach a stile in the hedge opposite. Cross and go towards a double telegraph pole, passing it to reach a stile in a stone wall. Cross on to a minor road, and cross to another stile. Cross and walk alongside Sudburn Beck, going through nine small, narrow fields. After about $^1/_2$ mile climb some steps to reach the main A688 road to Sudburn Bridge. Cross it with care, and go over the old road to a stone stile. Cross and keep straight ahead to cross a wooden stile. Keep close to Sudburn Beck as it bends left. Soon a gate in a stone wall is reached; just below the white painted buildings of Snotterton Hall on your right. Go through the gate ahead to reach a footpath over Sudburn Beck.

Turn left, cross the footbridge and climb between some thorn bushes to reach a large field. Continue along the left side of the field to the main A688 road. Cross the road to a wooden stile. Cross the stile and go diagonally left across the field ahead to another stile in the corner of a second field. Cross and go left along the side of the field to a third stile. Cross and bear right to another stile close to where a fence meets a stone wall. Cross it and keep close to the wall to some steps which will take you into the next field. Turn right to another stile. Cross and bear left to a gate close to some farm buildings. At the gate turn left along the road through Cleatlam village, passing the green and the pond on the right. Once past the buildings, turn left along a clear track to a wooden stile. Cross and bear diagonally right across an arable field, aiming for a stile in the stone wall ahead. Cross this stile and continue in the same direction to a wooden stile in a fence next to the road. Turn left along the road to the bridge over Sudburn Beck where there is a choice of routes: either retrace your steps to the Post Office or continue along the road into **Staindrop** passing the Comprehensive School.

## POINTS OF INTEREST:
**Staindrop** – With its large green surrounded by many fine historic buildings, Staindrop is one of the most attractive villages in Teesdale. It has been designated a conservation area in order to protect its character, and a number of the buildings have been sympathetically restored using traditional slates, not; pantiles and sash windows. The village is of Danish origin, the name meaning 'stony place'. It retained a charter for a weekly market and annual fair until 1796, when Barnard Castle became the areas market town.

## REFRESHMENTS:
*The Wheatsheaf Inn*, Staindrop (tel no: 0833 60280).

# Walk 28    BISHOP AUCKLAND AND ESCOMB    4m (6.5km)

Maps: OS Sheets Landranger 92 & 93; Pathfinder NZ 12/13 & NZ 22/32.

*Very easy, mainly riverside, walking.*

Start: The Bondgate Car Park, Bishop Auckland.

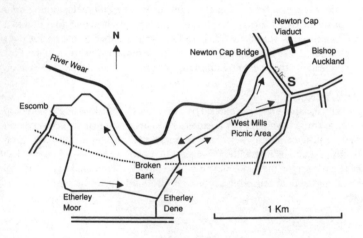

From the car park turn right along North Bondgate. Continue into High Bondgate, cross the A689, turn left into West Road and then right into Hexham Street. At the far end, go down a path between allotments to come out almost opposite West Mill Picnic Area. Go left along a road, and where it ends cross a stile and take the path ahead, with the River Wear on your right, through scrub and gorse: the path is marked with white posts. Where the path splits take the right fork, and continue westwards to where a marker post directs you back to the river. Go upstream along the river bank for a few yards and cross a little feeder on a footbridge. Keep by the river through four pastures, then cross a stile and bear first left, then right over scrub to reach a lane near an electricity sub-station. Go along the lane into the small village of **Escomb**. Leave the village along Bede Close at the north-eastern end of the village. Cross 2 stiles and turn right, southwards, close to the edge of the next two stiled fields. Bridge the Weardale Railway and maintaining the same direction, go up the next two stiled fields into Green Lane. Here you have a choice of routes. The shorter way is left at a shed marked 'Beware of The Guard Dog' and across fields using kissing gates and stiles to a terrace of cottages called Primrose Villa, AD 1874, and marked 'Primrose Hill' on the OS map. For the longer route, go along Green Lane to Etherley Moor. Turn left along the B6282 on a wayside footpath to Etherley Dene. Turn left opposite the Mason's Arms and go along an unsurfaced lane to the Primrose Villa terrace where the routes re-join. Continue down the lane and back over the Weardale Railway. Cross a stile on the far side and go right, along a path to Brocken Bank where the route split on the outward journey. To return to Bishop Auckland either take the route followed on the outward journey, or from the West Mills Picnic Area, continue along the riverside road to the B689 and go right along it back to Bishop Auckland.

POINTS OF INTEREST:
**Escomb** – The village church is the oldest complete Saxon church in England, and one of the best examples of Anglo-Saxon architecture in Western Europe. It was built in the second half of the 7th century with stone taken from the Roman fort of Binchester.

REFRESHMENTS:
Bishop Auckland is well endowed with hotels, pubs and cafés.
*The Saxon Inn*, Escomb (tel no: 0388 662256).
*The Mason's Arms*, Etherley Dene (tel no: 0388 602977).

# Walk 29      CASSOP VALE      4m (6.5km)

Maps: OS Sheets Landranger 93; Pathfinder NZ 23/33.

*A good all seasons walk in limestone country, with lots of birds for company.*

Start: Cassop Colliery Post Office.

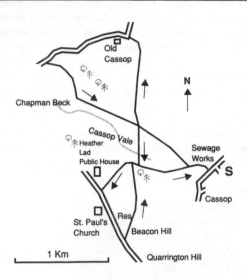

From the Post Office cross to the footpath opposite and go along it, turning right past the sewage works. Continue to a crossroads. Turn right and climb to the hilltop from where you can see Signing Bank: from it pilgrims first saw Durham Cathedral and made the sign of the cross. Continue to Old Cassop village: from its eastern end the views over central and west Durham are excellent. Go through the village, leaving it downhill. Take the track on the left to reach, at the bottom, some large lumps of burnt shale, all that remains of **Cassop Vale** Colliery. On reaching a wagonway first turn left, then right at a crossroads. Cross the Vale bottom, go over a stile, cross a beck and turn right through woods. The Heather Lad public house is seen on the horizon: aim to the left of it to join a minor road. Turn left along the road, soon passing, on your right, St Pauls', the Parish Church of Cassop Cum Quarrington. The local, extensive, quarries have been in use since the 13th century and lime from hereabouts was almost certainly used to cement the stones of Durham Cathedral. On approaching the village turn left on to the path to Beacon Hill, from where the quarry faces of Coxhoe Quarry can be seen. Continue ahead, crossing two stiles to reach a wagonway. Turn left along the wagonway which was once used for carrying coal. At the bottom of the shallow vale turn right, passing some more old quarries whose scars are becoming mellowed through weathering and the growth of natural vegetation. Along here blue tits and goldfinches are frequently seen, as are yellow hammers during the summer months. After reaching the top of a hill continue to Cassop, returning along the same route past the sewage works used on the outward part of the walk.

POINTS OF INTEREST:
**Cassop Vale** – The Vale was once the bed of a shallow lagoon into which flowed rivers carrying large amounts of calcium and magnesium salts. When the waters evaporated in the high temperatures of that time vast deposits of dolomite and calcium were created. Distortions of the earth's crust raised this dolomite sea-bed which retreating glaciers ripped and serrated. Man has quarried it extensively, farmed its topsoil and mined through and below it looking for coal.

REFRESHMENTS:
*The Heather Lad*, Cassop.

# Walk 30    LITTLETOWN AND ELEMORE WOOD    4m (6.5km)

Maps: OS Sheets Landranger 88; Pathfinder NZ 24/34.

*An easy, enjoyable walk.*

Start: At 340434, The Duke of York, Littletown.

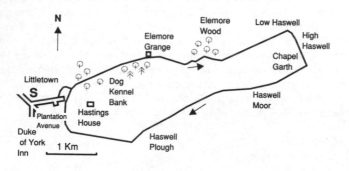

From The Duke of York go northwards along Plantation Avenue and, at the top end of it, among some garages, cross a stile on your left and take the path ahead towards a wood. Cross a bridge and turn left past a gloomy surround of spruce trees below which nothing much grows. Continue between pillars which once supported the gates to Elemore Hall, now a County Council Special School that can be glimpsed through parkland. The path continues through woodland and keeps straight ahead, edging the wood on the right. Soon, on your left, a newly-laid hedge edges the left side of the path for almost $\frac{1}{2}$ mile, beyond which the buildings of Elemore Grange are passed. Arched to take hay, horses cars and cattle, these buildings were built to serve the needs of farming methods no longer used today. Just past Elemore Grange more spruce trees are passed, but these are spread thinner and have enough space in which to grow as Nature intended. They add a touch of Christmas to the scene. When the path bifurcates take the fork to the left of a stream to reach a field well sheltered by trees. Continue northwards, edging the wood on your left and ignoring paths going left and right, moving steadily uphill towards Low Haswell, seen ahead. On reaching it turn right to reach the hilltop, from where the surrounding countryside is seen in panoramic splendour. The hidden remains of Chapel Garth lie buried to the east of the hilltop viewpoint. Also just east of the viewpoint is the road to **Haswell Moor**. Turn right along it, and bear right at the end of a wood. Continue southwards, aiming for the houses at Sherburn Hill, seen on the horizon. At one time an ugly pit heap blocked the view but careful landscaping has transformed the area into pleasant grassland. On reaching a road turn right. Walk until you reach the drive to Hastings House on your right. Turn right and immediately go left along a path towards some beech trees. Where a path comes to meet you from the left, take it, retracing your steps to The Duke of York.

POINTS OF INTEREST:
**Haswell Moor** – Home to 200 Canadian Holstein Cows, bred for their record milk yields.

REFRESHMENTS:
*The Duke of York*, Littletown (tel no: 091 372 0440).

## Walk 31    MIDDLETON-ONE-ROW AND LOW DINSDALE    4¹/₄m (7km)

Maps: OS Sheets Landranger 93; Pathfinder NZ 21/31.

*A good helping of woodland and riverside walking.*

Start: The Davenport Hotel, Middleton-One-Row.

From the hotel cross the road and follow the path which descends diagonally to the River Tees – across which lies Yorkshire. Continue upstream, crossing a bridge with a single handrail to join **Pountey's Lane**. Continue past a car park on your right to Dinsdale Spa. Pass the Spa, keeping on the clear, woodland path. Cross two brick bridges and descend to the edge of the wood. Continue across the field ahead, aiming for a clearly seen electricity pole and Low Dinsdale.

Leave the field through a kissing gate on to a minor road. A detour left, along the road – which leads to Over Dinsdale Hall on the Yorkshire bank – will be rewarded with good views of the River Tees. Those not making the detour should turn right along the road past Dinsdale Manor, on the right. The house is called SIWARD because in Norman times the Siward family settled there. Being French and living beside the

70

Tees they called themselves *Sur Tees*, and Surtees is a well known family name in County Durham today. A row of chestnut trees enhances Siward, whilst Manor Farm opposite owes much of its charm to some stone water troughs and a strangely weather-beaten garden wall.

Turn right at a footpath sign under an ash tree and follow a clear path that edges, and goes above, the woods you have just come through. From here Dinsdale School and Middleton-One-Row can be seen and, on clear days, the North York Moors and the Cleveland Hills are visible. The walk now goes between the greens of a golf course to reach a surfaced road. Turn right, passing between the buildings of Dinsdale Park, a special residential school run by the County Council. Avoid the gardens of Bath Villa, and regain the outward route at Dinsdale Spa. Turn left, briefly, and left again along Pountey's Lane. Turn right along Church Lane, going past St Laurence's Church with its Saxon sundial to return to Middleton-One-Row.

POINTS OF INTEREST:
**Pountey's Lane** – The name comes from the Roman *Pons Tesie*. The site of Pountey's Bridge is just below the car park. A mound on Tower Hill, to the right of the line of the walk as the small bridge is crossed, may have been built to defend the bridge.
In 1789 men looking for coal sources along the banks of the River Tees broke through a layer of rock and released a stream of sulphurous water. At that time mineral springs were thought to be a cure for all ailments. Although never as fashionable as Buxton or Bath, Dinsdale Spa was thought by the Stockton and Darlington Railway Company to have potential, and they built Dinsdale Station to accommodate the anticipated passenger traffic.

REFRESHMENTS:
*The Davenport Hotel*, Middleton-One-Row (tel no: 0325 332255).

# Walk 32    HAMSTERLEY AND DIPTON WOODS    4¼m (7km)

Maps: OS Sheets Landranger 88; Pathfinder NZ 05/15.

*A very pleasant walk, mostly through delightful woodland.*

Start: At 154536, Dipton car park, next to Collierley School.

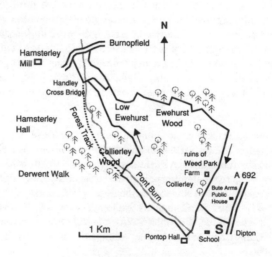

From the car park at Dipton, a late 19th-century mining village, go left for 20 yards along the A692 towards Burnopfield and turn left along a track between two houses. Go downhill, between allotments, and cross a stile. On reaching a T-junction, go left along a disused railway line. Cross a stile at a point where an embankment has been used to turn a stream into a pond to provide a suitable habitat for frogs, and beyond the pond go right, northwards, close to the stream on your right. On reaching the wood ahead turn left on to a track for a few yards, then go right, through conifers, and continue northwards to where silver birch are colonising an area where earlier trees had been burned down. Go right near a railway sleeper bridge, crossing another bridge and following a broad track to the edge of a wood. Go left, along the edge, re-entering the wood and crossing Handley Cross Bridge on to the drive of **Hamsterley Hall**. A short cut goes right just before the bridge. Turn right at the lodge and continue along the road towards Burnopfield for almost $1/_4$ mile. Turn right into a wood at a footpath sign.

The Woodland Trust, a charitable body which buys deciduous woodland to preserve and improve it, owns this wood. Follow the clear path which bridges a stream. Soon after the path curves left, southwards, leaving the wood over a stile into a field. Continue along the left side of the field, crossing two facing stiles, to reach Low Ewehurst Farm. Follow the farm road to the left and leave it at the next bend, going right over a stile. Bear left, at first close to Ewehurst Wood on your left then entering it over a stile. Go through the wood, turning left, then right along a path that soon curves right to a crossing of paths. Go left to the wood's edge. Turn right along a facing path and cross a stile. Continue to a junction of paths. Turn right and continue, crossing stiles, passing, on your right, the remains of Weed Park Farm. Cross further stiles to meet the outward journey route. Turn left and re-trace your steps to the start of the walk.

POINTS OF INTEREST:
The early owners of Pontop Hall, seen on your left where you turn right beyond the frog pond, had the Norman names of De Gourley and De Claxton. The Bulmers, who also lived there, were Saxon. For several centuries Pontop Hall was owned by Catholics and was often seized by the crown when the owners were suspected of 'Popery'.

**Hamsterley Hall** – The hall was built in 1762 for a member of the family that owned Pontop Hall. A later owner, R S Surtees, famous author of the *Jorrocks Fox Hunting Tales*, built Handley Cross Bridge with the profits from his best selling novel *Handley Cross*.

## Walk 33  NEVILLES CROSS AND BEARPARK HALL FARM  4½m (7km)

Maps: OS Sheets Landranger 88; Pathfinder NZ 24/34.

*A fine walk with a nice sense of history.*

Start: At 262420, Nevilles Cross, on the outskirts of Durham City.

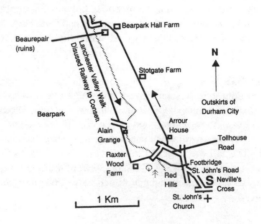

At Nevilles Cross, opposite St John's Church, there is the caged stump of an old cross that commemorates one of the fiercest **battles** ever fought between England and Scotland. From it go along St John's Road, turning left at the far end to join the A167. Turn right, bridging the railway line at Red Hills cutting. Cross the A167 at the first footbridge and continue along it to the Pot and Glass Inn. Turn left along Tollhouse Road. At the end of the terrace on the right, turn right and go uphill to Arbour House Farm. From there, continue across open country in the same direction along a clear track. To your left there are good views of the Browney Valley. Leave the track under a line of pylons, going left, through a kissing gate, and right along another track passing Shotgate Farm on the right. This track was used by monks en route to Beau

74

Repaire, the ruins of which can be seen on your left as Bearpark Hall Farm is reached. Beau Repaire was a country retreat for the Prior and monks of Durham Cathedral. Originally a small cattle farm, it was added to over the years, and by the mid-13th century the estate had grown to encompass most of the lower Browney valley.

Beyond Bearpark Hall (the name Bearpark is a corruption of Beau Repaire) the path descends to cross the River Browney on a substantial bridge, then climbs to join the old railway line to Consett, now converted into the Lanchester Valley Walk. Turn left along the track from where the views of ruinous Beau Repaire across the valley on your left are good, while to the right is the site of the old Bearpark Collieries, now completely landscaped. Where the road from Bearpark village to Durham intersects the track, cross it with care and continue along the old railway, passing Aldin Grange Farm on your left. About $^1/_2$ mile beyond the farm, just after you have walked under some pylons, turn left along a farm track to Baxter Wood Farm. Bear left there, along the main track through the farm yard to the left of some old farm buildings. Beyond, the track becomes a surfaced road that crosses the River Browney. Turn right immediately after crossing the bridge, through a gap in the fence, and go along a pleasant riverside path through Baxter Wood. The path now goes left, through a gap in the fence, away from the river, to skirt a disused quarry. Continue along the edge of a field, exiting over a stile. Follow a wide gravel track, climbing uphill, and turn right past some railway cottages. A little further on the track curves left, then right to reach the A167.

Cross the road on the footbridge used on the outward journey. Turn right along the road to a point just short of a petrol station, where you turn left up to St John's Road. Turn right to return to the monument.

### POINTS OF INTEREST:

**Battle** – During the summer of 1346, while Edward III was across the Channel, a Scottish army under King David II marched through Cumbria and Tynedale. Queen Phillipa, having mobilised an English army, was joined by northern nobles and the Bishop's Palatine army. The Scots reached Beau Repaire on 16th October and the following day, after a skirmish, the English and Scottish armies met at Nevilles Cross. The Scots were heavily defeated, King David was found hiding under a bridge at Aldin Grange, his reflection in the River Browney betraying him and he spent many years a prisoner in the Tower of London.

### REFRESHMENTS:

Hotels, pubs and cafés in Durham City.

# Walk 34 SHERBURN, SHINCLIFFE AND PALACE GREEN 4¹/₂m (7km)

Maps: OS Sheets Landranger 88; Pathfinder NZ 24/34.

*A most interesting walk that links 5 bridges constructed by the Prince Bishops.*

Start: At 307417, Sherburn Hospital Gatehouse, to where a regular bus service runs from Durham City.

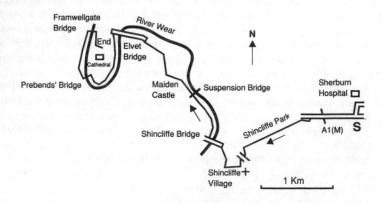

From **Sherburn Hospital** gate house go along the road directly opposite and at the next road junction turn right, towards Durham, and cross the motorway bridge. From here the Cathedral is directly ahead. Once over the motorway take the second left, signposted 'Private Road to Manor Farm', which is a public footpath. The gravel path follows an old colliery wagonway. Where the farm road curves to the left go right into an area of woodland called Shincliffe Park. Go along this straight, and very fine, silvan walk, and where the wood ends, bear left along the field edge to the main A177. Cross this busy road with care, going slightly right and climbing some stone steps to reach a level path through the churchyard. Go past the west end of the church to reach Shincliffe village green. Follow the road around and back to the A177, reaching it at the Rose Tree Filling Station. Cross the road, again with care, and turn left to Durham, crossing the River Wear on Shincliffe Bridge, a Palatine crossing point. Walter Skirlaw, the great 14th-century bridge-building Bishop, built a bridge at Shincliffe to replace an earlier structure: the present one was built in 1826. Once across, turn right to follow a riverside path along a raised embankment and under the modern suspension bridge. If you have difficulty using the path under the suspension bridge go through the wooden gate, and, with the kind permission of the University, continue along the riverbank, passing the steeply wooded slopes of Maiden Castle on the left. At the end of the woods follow a well-trodden path to the left which skirts a sports field. Where the track joins a metalled road turn left and continue along it to the main road. Here turn right and walk down into Durham along Old Elvet with its fine Georgian houses. Go straight ahead at the traffic lights, and continue along the pedestrian street and across **Elvet Bridge**. Once over the bridge go down steps on its right-hand side and turn right under its landlocked arch to follow a riverside path. Go under Kingsgate Bridge and past Count's House to take the upper path to Prebends Bridge. This lovely bridge replaced an earlier one in 1778: from it you have one of the classic views of the Cathedral. Cross the bridge and turn right along the lower riverbank to cross the river again at Framwellgate Bridge. The original bridge here was built in 1128 by Bishop Ranulph Flambard. It was rebuilt in the early 15th century, rebuilt in 1856 and is now pedestrianised. Turn down steps to the right and bear left, climbing up the Broken Walls Walk. Just before the Cathedral, turn left up a narrow lane called Windy Gap to reach the Palace Green where this fine walk ends.

### POINTS OF INTEREST:

**Sherburn Hospital** – Founded by Bishop Pudsey in 1181 to house a community of 65 lepers. In time, because of neglect, the building fell into disrepair and around 1300 was largely destroyed by the Scots.

**Elvet Bridge** – The original bridge was built in Bishop Pudsey's time, around 1160, and contributed to Durham's prosperity. There was a religious house at each end of it. In 1495 Bishop Fox had it repaired and at the beginning of the 18th century it was widened.

### REFRESHMENTS:

Hotels, pubs and cafés in Durham City.

# Walk 35  DURHAM CITY AND HOUGHALL CIRCULAR  4½m (7km)
Maps: OS Sheets Landranger 88; Pathfinder NZ 24/34.
*An easy walk along the River Wear.*
Start: Durham City Market Place.

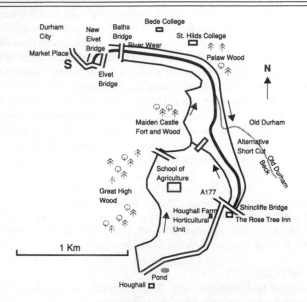

From the Market Place go along Fleshergate, then left down Elvet to Elvet Bridge. At the optician's, descend Elvet Steps to the towpath. Turn left, going behind Brown's Boathouse and under New Elvet Bridge. Continue past Baths Bridge from where the retrospective view of ancient Durham City, dominated by its castle and cathedral is superb. Keep along the riverside towpath, with the Colleges of St Bede and St Hild over on your left and the old Racecourse across the river – which thereabouts becomes the famous Regatta Course. Where the towpath ends, enter Pelaw Wood, still on a riverside path. On leaving the wood, ignore the path on your left, and go diagonally left over a rough pasture to a track which curves left by a disused railway embankment. Turn right between the supports of a demolished railway bridge to cross two stiles and a metal bridge over Old Durham Beck. Turn left and, by aiming between football fields on the far bank, take a route that reaches the River Wear at a suspension bridge.

Instead of crossing the bridge go left along the edge of a field to join a riverside path which becomes a cart track and reaches the A177 near the Rose Tree Inn (on the far side of the road). Turn right – unless you have visited the pub when it is left – and cross Shincliffe Bridge over the River Wear. After 30 yards, turn left into an unsignposted lane. Now enter a car park on your left: this is the start of the two mile long **Houghall Discovery Trail** which coincides with our walk for some distance. From the car park enter Shincliffe Bridge Wood along a path which passes the first of nine information boards, to rejoin the lane near the **Houghall Farm Horticultural Unit** (on your right). Continue along the lane as far as some Houghall staff houses, and there turn right and follow yellow arrows along a lane. Go over a stile and along the right side of a holly hedge to the top of a field. Cross a corner stile into Great High Wood. Turn right along a path running just inside the wood to reach the A177. Cross to enter Main Castle Wood. Take the path round the base of the wooded knoll on which Maiden Castle once stood, and turn left on to a riverside path leading into Green Lane. Turn right to reach the river beside Durham Amateur Rowing Club. Turn left along the river bank to Baths Bridge, and cross it to complete this delightful walk along the outward route.

POINTS OF INTEREST:
**Houghall Discovery Trail** – A woodland to right of the Discovery Trail was once an ugly pit heap. In the 1920's Durham County Council camouflaged it with trees, making it the first industrial eyesore in the country to be reclaimed. Further along the trail are Houghall Railway Sidings and all that is now left of an abandoned colliery and its attendant pit village.
**Houghall Farm Horticultural Unit** – The Unit stands on the site of the water works which supplied Durham City with its first tap water.

REFRESHMENTS:
There are plenty of hotels, pubs and cafés in Durham City.
*The Rose Tree Inn*, Shincliffe (tel no: 0913 868512).

# Walk 36   FLATTS WOOD   4½m (7km)

Maps: OS Sheets Landranger 92; Outdoor Leisure 31.

*A nice walk, particularly in spring and summer, along the River Tees and Percy Beck.*

Start: The Castle Gates, Barnard Castle.

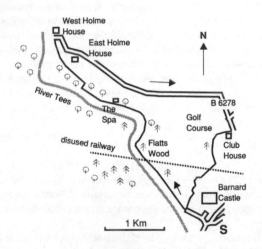

From the Castle Gates, **Barnard Castle**, follow the path signposted 'To the Woods' and, ignoring the bridge over the River Tees, continue upstream, crossing Percy Beck on a footbridge into Flatts Wood. The path continues past the supports of the dismantled viaduct that once carried the Darlington to Kirkby Stephen railway line. Descend to the riverside and climb a rock face up a stone stairway which was hewn in Victorian times to enable visitors to visit the sulphurous waters that once gushed from nearby springs. These springs dried up long ago, but the remains of the bath house can still be seen in the undergrowth. The path ends at a field gate so continue close to a wall alongside the wood through a gate on your right. Climb steeply uphill. At the top of the wooded slope turn left along a path leading to West Holme House, the more distance of the two whitewashed Raby Farms seen ahead. At the farm road turn right towards East Holme. Continue along the farm road, which crosses flat farmland, passing, on your left, Knott Hill, on which can be seen strip lynchets, the remains of a medieval farming system. The Ancient village of Marwood was sited on Knott Hill, with its naturally drained slopes, at a time when the surrounding land was waterlogged woodland. There is a golf course on your right. At the B6278 turn right. Follow the road to where, after crossing Percy Beck, you can turn right in front of the Club House. Go through a kissing gate and along a path into a wooded valley. Keep to the beckside path all the way through the wood where, especially in winter, the series of waterfalls adds a touch of drama to the scene. These woods are private and the paths are not rights of way in the legal sense, Ray Estates, the owners of the land, having an agreement with the District Council who maintain the paths, whereby the public are permitted to walk through and enjoy the pleasures this lovely wooded valley has to offer. Go under a disused stone viaduct and over several footbridges, following a descending path back to the River Tees. From there retrace your steps to the Castle Gates.

## POINTS OF INTEREST:

**Barnard Castle** – The Castle was built between 1112 and 1132. Both castle and town take their name from Barnard Baliol, son of Guy, who came to England with William the Conqueror.

Directly to your back as you walk alongside the golf course, and on the horizon, is the whale backed ridge of Mickle Fell, the highest point in County Durham. Before the 1974 boundary changes Mickle Fell was the highest point in Yorkshire.

## REFRESHMENTS:

Hotels, pubs and cafés in Barnard Castle.

Walk 37 **MIDDLETON-IN-TEESDALE AND WYTHES HILL** 5m (8km)
Maps: OS Sheets Landranger 92; Outdoor Leisure 31.
*A superb hill walk, much of it on the Pennine Way.*
Start: The Fountain, Middleton-in-Teesdale.

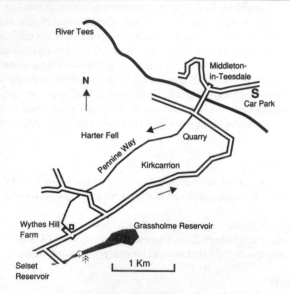

From the fountain in Middleton-in-Teesdale (see Note to Walk 5) go southwards along the B6277, crossing the Tees. When the side road to Holwick is reached turn right, along it, then left as signposted. Go through a gate and follow a bridleway up a pasture, having now joined the Pennine Way. Continue, climbing steadily, parallel to a wall on your left, and go through a metal gate in a facing wall. Keep climbing across the rough pasture ahead and where the path divides, go right crossing a water course on a wooden bridge. Continue upwards to a gate in a facing fence and where the path splits a second time, go right again, diagonally, on a bearing of 261°. Soon the path curves left to reach a gate in a facing wall, just left of a corner with a fence. Go through and cross the field ahead along a clear path. Go through a metal gate in a facing wall, and go right, parallel to the wall on your right, to a stile in a facing wall. Pass a stone building on your right and cross a white-washed stile left of a gate. Cross a rough pasture diagonally left, to reach a cairn and a PW sign near a broken wall. From here there are excellent views into Lunedale, with Grassholme Reservoir to your left and Selset a little further on. Following a descending path to a gate with a yellow arrow on your right. Go through and continue along a broad track passing, on the right, a small enclosure with trees. Soon after passing a field house on the left, cross a stile in a facing wall near a gate. Continue along a clear track and cross another stile near a gate. Now go diagonally left to a waymarked gateway in a wall and go through it to join a clear, unsurfaced road. After 100 yards leave the road diagonally right to cross a stile in the wall ahead. Descend diagonally left to a walled lane just in front of Wythes Hill Farm seen ahead. Ford a beck at the lane end, enter the lane, climb steeply up it and continue along it, past the farm. Turn right, then left to reach the B6276 and leave the Pennine Way. Go left along the road for a very pleasant $1^1/_2$ miles, passing, on your left, the lane end to Greengates Farm, to reach a signposted path on your left. The path climbs close to a wall on the left for a while, then bears right away from the wall. It next curves left to climb past the south-east side of **Kirkcarrion** to reach a wall stile. Cross this stile and continue downhill, north-eastwards, pulling away from the wall on your right. Soon, as the wall changes direction, you draw closer to it again. Continue to the point where, just past a metal gate, the outward route branched right, and from there retrace your steps back to the fountain.

POINTS OF INTEREST:
**Kirkcarrion** – A familiar Upper Teesdale landmark. It is a walled plantation on the top of a hillock and the site of a tumulus. It is reputed to be haunted.

REFRESHMENTS:
Hotels, pubs and cafés in Middleton-in-Teesdale.

# Walk 38   St John's Chapel and Middlehope Shield Mine

5m (8km)

Maps: OS Sheets Landranger 92 & 87; Outdoor Leisure 31.

*Five miles of fairly easy walking, part of it along the Weardale Way.*

Start: St John's Chapel village.

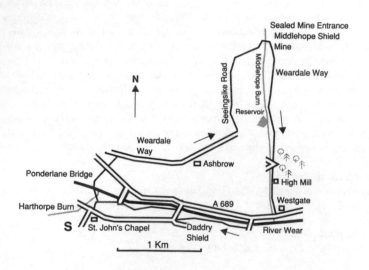

From St John's Chapel go along the lane behind the Village Hall. Turn left over Harthope Burn at the cottages, then go right by a public footpath sign and along a paved path over Ponderlane Bridge. Continue up the side of the field ahead, climb some railed steps and cross the next field to a signposted stile. Cross the road immediately ahead, take the signposted path across two pastures and climb steeply up the third to another road. Turn right along this road which, as far as Ash Brow Farm, coincides with the Weardale Way (see Note to Walk 60). After 1 mile the road ends at a junction with Seeingsike Road, an ancient, walled, lead miners' track. Turn left, following directions from a footpath sign, and climb on to the fell. Where the track bifurcates after almost $^1/_2$ mile, take the right fork and descend steeply down the valley side. Go through a gate at the bottom, ford Middlehope Burn and pass a gated mine on your left. Follow the path southwards close to the burn on your right. The path passes through the ruins of Middlehope Shield Mine, which are dangerous to explore. Continue through a wood to the extensive industrial remains of Slit Mine with its capped mine shaft. The shaft was one of the deepest in the north at 585 feet. Once past the old buildings and the dressing floors, enter **Slitts Wood**, a nature reserve. Cross and recross a burn on footbridges, and go through a kissing gate into the private garden of High Mill, an old corn mill. Keeping to the path, pass Chapel Cottages and enter Westgate. Turn right along the main street and just past Westgate Filling Station turn left along a lane to cross the River Wear on a footbridge. Continue along the road past the supports of a railway bridge, and take the signposted path on the right which goes westwards across three fields to Windyside. Just past a terrace of cottages, turn right, then left over a footbridge and into a pasture. Ignoring the riverside route, which is not a right of way, climb up to a gate in the wall above a wood. Go through and follow the path over a pasture. Cross a stile in the wall on your right and take the stiled path to Daddry Shield. Now turn right along the A689 to Daddry Shield Bridge, and take the signposted path on the left. Go down some steps over a footbridge to follow the riverside path for $^1/_2$ mile to Huntshield. Turn left along the lane back to St John's Chapel.

POINTS OF INTEREST:
**Slitts Wood** – Noted for its natural beauty and its bird life.

REFRESHMENTS:
There are several pubs in St John's Chapel.

# Walk 39     LUMLEY PARK AND CASTLE     5m (8km)

Maps: OS Sheets Landranger 88; Pathfinder NZ 25.35.

*A walk through interesting woodlands, with good views of parkland and riverside. Best done in spring.*

Start: Lumley New Bridge, Chester-le-Street.

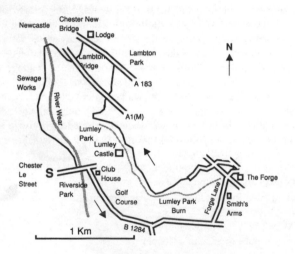

   From the parking area near **Lumley New Bridge** cross the River Wear and go right, along the B1248 from where there are good views of the south front of **Lumley Castle**. Continue past the golf course on your left, and soon after passing some homes for aged mineworkers, turn left along Forge Lane to the bridge which carries the A1(M) across Lumley Park Burn. Go under the bridge where, before crossing the burn, a short diversion can be made to the site of a forge: the mill races and sluices can still be seen. Returning to Forge Lane, cross the burn, climb some steps and turn left. Go left again over a bridge crossing the motorway. Continue past Lumley Park Farm and cross the track of an old wagonway that was built to carry coal from one of the Lumley's pits. The way is through Lumley Park Wood, passing, but not crossing, the Lamb Bridge, which provides a private rear entrance to the castle.

Just past the castle a walled garden is passed, beyond which is Garden House, on your left. Just past the house there is a stile. Go right here, along a lane and across a field to another motorway bridge.

Cross and continue past Lumley Lodge, one of several Victorian cottages built for estate workers, to reach the Chester Road which separates the Lumley and Lambton estates. Go left along it, using a roadside path, to Lambton Bridge. Cross and turn left on to a riverside footpath. Follow the path upstream and under the bridge that carries the A1(M) over the River Wear. This bridge was built over dry land where ground conditions were more stable than on the river banks. Once the construction was complete the river was diverted to flow beneath it. The flat, riverside land across which the route goes is almost all artificial, created from domestic waste over the last 60 years. Continue upstream, crossing Longburn on a footbridge at its confluence with the River Wear, and stay on the path back to Lumley New Bridge and the start of the walk.

POINTS OF INTEREST:
**Lumley New Bridge** – Built in 1914 to replace a ferry and a toll footbridge.
**Lumley Castle** – Build in the 14th century, but re-constructed in 1721 by Sir John Vanburgh, the architect of Blenheim Palace.
The bridge downstream of Lambton Bridge is Chester New Bridge, which despite its name is 600 years old, the same age as Lumley Castle

REFRESHMENTS:
Hotels, cafés and pubs in Chester-le-Street.

Walk 40     THE PRINCE BISHOPS CIRCULAR     5m (8km)
Maps: OS Sheets Landranger 93; Pathfinder NZ 22/32 & 23/33.
*A pleasant circular along the Gaunless valley and down 800
years of ecclesiastical history.*
Start: Bishop Auckland Market Place.

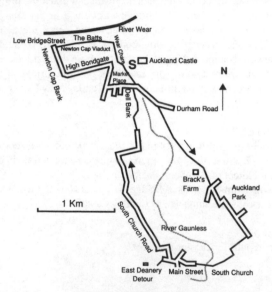

Leave the Market Place entrance to **Auckland Castle** along Durham Road, which, as
it descends to cross the Gaunless Valley offers some good views of the castle grounds.
Stay on the road as it climbs out of the valley and, opposite a red-brick house with
balconies, turn right at a footpath sign and follow a metalled path across a field towards
a wood. Continue with the edge of the wood on your right, and cross the farm road to
Brack's Farm, which is also on your right. Go through a wicket gate ahead and continue
along the right edge of a field to exit at a by-pass near Auckland Park village. Cross
the road at a pedestrian refuge. Continue in the same direction along Douglas Crescent,
passing a Methodist Chapel on a tight double bend, and keep on the road for about
300 yards. There, just short of a factory, turn right over two stiles. Keep close to the
right edge of the field ahead as far as a stile on your right. Cross the stile to join a

88

surfaced path to the railway embankment, seen ahead. Go through this, under a bridge, to join another surfaced path going straight ahead. Where the path bifurcates, turn right to reach South Church. Turn left at the end of Atherton Terrace, then go right, over the river Gaunless and cross the green to **St Andrew Auckland** church. From the church gate cross the main road and turn right briefly. Here, go left for a short detour along a path that crosses the river Gaunless on a metal bridge that hides an earlier stone one, and climbs a hill on top of which sits the East Deanery, with West Deanery behind. Retrace your steps to the main road, cross and join a footpath beside the west wall of the church, leaving it at a lych-gate by turning left and crossing a footbridge. Now turn right along the A6072, going under a railway bridge. Beyond the bridge, take the third turning on the right, along Woodlands Road. At the bottom turn left along a track which quickly turns right, along a fenced path, then left, past a school on the left, then sharp right, down some steps. Turn left at the bottom, along a riverside track, to reach a bridge. Turn left, uphill, cross the main road at the top and continue along it to Newgate Street. Turn right along this pedestrian shopping mall, continue along the west side of the Market Place and turn left into North Bondgate. Keeping to the right side of it, go uphill, along High Bondgate, then down the main road as far as Newton Gap Bridge. Do not cross. Instead, turn right, down steps, and go along the riverside, known hereabouts as the Batts. Leave at Batts Terrace, a row of terraced houses. Detour left, along Binchester Road to see the hillside, pinnacled chapel of Auckland Castle. Retrace your steps to Batts Terrace and turn left, uphill, back to the Market Place, ready, perhaps, to explore the Bishop's Park (see Note to Walk 15) which is open to the public.

POINTS OF INTEREST:

**Auckland Castle** – Bishop Pudsey built the castle around 1183. Bec added medieval chapels and as it became a favourite country residence of the Bishops others made their own improvements. The chapels were destroyed during Cromwell's predominance and the castle was sold. After the Restoration it was returned to its rightful owner, Bishop Cosin, who spent a fortune restoring it.

**St Andrew Auckland** – In the church there is an effigy of a knight with his feet resting on a boar. The story is that a local knight, Pollard, killed a boar that had been terrorising the area. He was rewarded with as much land as he could ride around while the Bishop was at dinner in Auckland Castle.

REFRESHMENTS:

Hotels and pubs in Bishop Auckland.
*The Prince Bishop Restaurant*, South Church (tel no: 0388 662128).

# Walk 41  MIDDLETON-IN-TEESDALE AND HUDESHOPE VALLEY  6m (9.5km)

Maps: OS Sheets Landranger 92; Outdoor Leisure 31.

*A good mix of road, woodland and field paths.*

Start: The Memorial Fountain, Middleton-in-Teesdale.

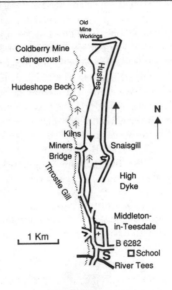

From the fountain cross the road, going past the war memorial and along Wesley Terrace. At the end, take the footpath uphill past a beech hedge that hides a churchyard. Stay on the path as it turns left, then right into a field. Within a few yards go over a stile on your left into a courtyard and continue diagonally right up two steps and along a narrow passage to a road. Turn right for about 60 yards, then go left along another road into woods. Almost immediately go right, through trees on a rough track. This track is called King's Walk and is not a public right of way: Raby Estates have granted permission for people to walk along it. The track climbs through pine and beech trees and curves right up a short, steep hill to a barn on the right. Bear left with the track as it continues upwards, through trees, and descends to cross Snaisgill Beck over a wooden bridge. Continue left, along a narrow path, to a stone wall on the edge

90

of the plantation. Now turn right and follow the wall to a road. Turn left, passing some cottages and a retirement home. Stay with the road, which offers extensive views of moorland, valley and pasture. After $1^1/_2$ miles the road bends sharply to the left and descends through extensive old mine workings.

Ahead, and on the other side of the valley, are the remains of the large Coldberry Mine which, at its peak, produced vast quantities of lead ore for local smelt mills. The old mine working are highly dangerous and great care should be taken, even when on public rights of way.

As you go downhill leave the road through a gate on your left and, keeping close to a wall on your left, go down rough pasture. Pass a small gate on your left to reach a stile in the wall. Cross, and almost at once cross Marl Beck and continue downstream along a clear, grassy track. Pass a stone barn and go through old mining remains, beyond which you climb to a gate into the field ahead. Go through and, ignoring the clear track to your left, continue along a stone wall on your right. Keeping close to the wall for three fields to reach a stile on to a pleasant path through a plantation. Keep on the path as it drops steeply to cut across the front of the large, disused Skeers Quarry and then goes down past lime kilns to reach Beck Road. Turn left along the road for 1 mile to reach the main road. Turn right, downhill, past the church and along Middleton's Market Place to reach the fountain.

POINTS OF INTEREST:
The deep eroded gullies seen at the head of the valley are 'hushes'. They were formed by the sudden release of water stored behind earth dams which cleared out old diggings and exposed fresh veins of lead ore.

REFRESHMENTS:
Hotels, pubs and cafés in Middleton-in-Teesdale.

## Walk 42 **MIDDLETON-IN-TEESDALE AND MICKLETON** 6m (9.5km)
Maps: OS Sheets Landranger 92; Outdoor Leisure 31.

*A beautiful little walk with a bit of everything – field, fell, road, railway and riverside.*

Start: Middleton-in-Teesdale Car Park.

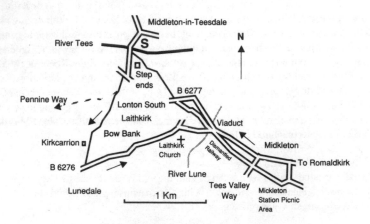

From the car park go left, down Bridge Street and along the B6277 to a road junction with a signpost reading 'Holwick 3 miles'. Turn right for a few yards, then left through a gate signposted with an acorn symbol. Continue straight ahead along a track, uphill, following the Pennine Way across Bowbank Fell. Go through a gate at the top of the first field, and at a bifurcation of tracks leave the Pennine Way and go left, uphill, and over a stile beside a gate. Pass the tree-covered Bronze Age burial site of the Brigantes Prince Caryn, Kirkcarrion – reputed to be haunted – above you on your right, and follow the track down to the B6276. Turn left down the road, passing Bowbank hamlet after 1 mile and, after a further ¹/₂ mile, reaching **Laithkirk**. Turn right, down Laithkirk Bank, go under the Lune Viaduct and turn right over Lune Bridge. Continue along the B6277 for a good ¹/₂ mile to reach Mickleton village where, opposite the Blacksmith's

Arms, turn right, up the road to the Mickleton Station Picnic Area. Turn right and continue along the disused Barnard Castle to Middleton-in-Teesdale line, crossing the Lune Viaduct. This section of the walk follows the Tees Valley Way, one of County Durham's most popular railway walks. At the western end of the reclaimed line, go along a field path, heading north-west, to reach Lonton South Farm. Now turn left along the B6277 as far as a signposted stile on your right. Cross and go down stiled pastures to Steps End Farm. The way now follows the riverside, upstream, to the County Bridge. Cross and go up Bridge Street back to the car park and the end of a grand, interesting walk.

POINTS OF INTEREST:
**Laithkirk** – The Queen Mother, before her marriage a Bowes-Lyon, with lots of local connections, visited Laithkirk Church during her honeymoon. Chapel House was once an inn and carries the inscription: *Good ale, Pipes and Tobacco. If by you go the Fault's in you and not in me.*

REFRESHMENTS:
There are hotels, pubs, a café and a fish and chip shop in Middleton-in-Teesdale.
*The Blacksmith's Arms,* Mickleton (tel no: 0833 40605).
*The Rose and Crown,* Mickleton (tel no: 0833 40381).

# Walk 43     COTHERSTONE AND BALDERSDALE     6m (9.5km)

Maps: OS Sheets Landranger 92; Outdoor Leisure 31.

*An easy walk along field and open moor paths, with a short road walk.*

Start: The village of Cotherstone.

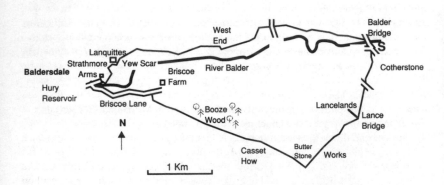

Park in the centre of the village and take the B6277 road towards Romaldkirk. On the outskirts of the village go over the Balder Bridge and immediately turn left through a hand gate displaying a footpath sign. Cross the field half right, passing through reeds, to a gap in some bushes on a slight rise. Pass through the gap and follow a good track to the top of the incline. Continue, with the river far below on your left, and cross a stile in a fence. Follow the field path through several more fields until the viaduct across the river comes into view. Head for a stile in a wire fence. Cross and head between telegraph poles to a concrete ladder stile leading on to a disused railway. Cross straight over to a similar stile, and then head towards a pair of telegraph poles. On reaching them aim for a field corner to the left, this time passing close to a single telegraph pole. Go through a gate to join a farm track and head towards West End

94

Farm. At the farm, go past the large building on the right, and at its end turn right to pass through two closely situated farm gates. In the field beyond, turn left at the wooden barn and follow the track across the centre. Go through a gate, and head to the left of the telegraph pole, aiming for a wooden structure erected in front of a stone wall stile. Negotiate the wooden structure and stile and cross some rough pasture. Head for an uprooted hawthorn tree and pass through a gate in the fence behind it. Keep the wire fence on your left and when it ends look for a gap in a stone wall on your right. Go through and follow the left-hand track to a wire fence. Follow the fence for a short way to a waymarked stone wall stile. Go over, scramble over the stream and up the opposite bank. Turn left at the top to pass through a broken down stone wall. Turn right to follow the stone wall towards a barn. Cross a stile in the wall to the left of the gate, and cross the field to a broken stone wall. From the wall corner head slightly left (south-west) to enter secluded woodland which leads down to a bridge. Cross and climb out of the woodland to a wall. Follow the yellow waymarker, keeping the wall on your right. On arriving at a barn, negotiate the metal gates to enter a walled green lane. Go along this lane, passing in front of Lanquittes holiday cottage, to reach a metalled road. In front of you can be seen the dam wall of the Hury reservoir (see Note to Walk 83). Cross the bridge and head up the road as far as the entrance to Booze Wood Farm. Turn right over the cattle grid and follow the farm road to its end. At the road end three signs indicate paths across the moor: take the centre one (which is the only bridleway) and follow it across the moor. The track is somewhat faint, but head east-south-east to reach the road in about a mile. Once on the road, turn left and follow it to Lance Bridge, reached just after the unfenced road is joined by a wall on the left. Just before the bridge a footpath sign on the left leads to a stone stile. After crossing the stile a good footpath leads to a wooden stile, beyond which is a meadow. Follow the footpath across the field to another wooden stile in the right-hand field corner. Head straight across the next field, cross a stile to the right of a wooden gate. The path now heads down to a stile in a stone wall. Go over this and a stone footbridge, aiming for the concrete ladder stiles which take you over the disused railway once more. The path now heads for a stone building about threequarters of the way down the field on the right-hand side. A small hand gate there leads into a lane. Turn left and enter Cotherstone.

REFRESHMENTS:
*The Red Lion Hotel,* Cotherstone (tel no: 0833 50236).

## Walk 44   MIDDLETON-ONE-ROW AND NEWSHAM HALL   6m (9.5km)

Maps: OS Sheets Landranger 93; Pathfinder NZ 21/31.

*A mainly riverside walk with pleasing distant views.*

Start: At 352123, The Front, Middleton-One-Row.

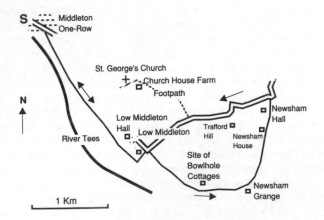

From The Front, beautifully sited some 60 feet above the River Tees and looking across the river into Yorkshire, turn left towards the eastern end of the village. Take the footpath that goes behind some houses, keeping between them and the river on your right, crossing stiles and descending along a well-worn path to enter a field. The path now continues parallel to the river and is well-defined. During the summer months it is much used by botanists because of the variety of wild plants to be found by the water's edge. A profusion of Rosebay Willow-herb, its white, fluffy seeds blowing in the autumn wind, guards the riverbank like an army of triffids. Before reaching the end of the riverside path, Low Middleton Hall, one time residence of Sir James Duff, Lieutenant of County Durham, is seen. Gathered around it like children around a school mistress is the small community of Low Middleton. Soon after passing an

96

ancient dovecote in a field to the left, slightly upstream of a fairly new embankment, climb on to the embankment. Walk along its top for a few yards and cross a stile on your left. Continue forward, away from the river, which, just downstream of this point, swings right. Cross a field close to a fence on the right, to reach a minor road at a sharp bend. There, turn right along a cart track, staying on it as it climbs most pleasantly to higher ground from where the views of the Cleveland Hills are good. Keep following the track as the terrain levels out, and when a fence is reached continue left along a green track to Newsham Grange, passing farm buildings on your right to reach a farm road. Turn left past Newsham House and Newsham Hall, on your left, to reach a minor road. Turn left along it for $1^1/_2$ miles: from the road there are good all round views. On returning to Low Middleton there is a choice of routes. Either return to the river and retrace your steps to Middleton-One-Row, or continue around the sharp bend and simply follow the road back to the start. The riverside walk is by far the better route in most respects, but should you choose the road route a point on the right is reached when a road branches off to Dinsdale. A short way along it a footpath leads off to the right to St George's Church, thought to be of Saxon origin. If church architecture is your forte, use the road route. Should your interest be more inclined to Natural History, the riverside way is for you. Either way, the old spa village of Middleton One-Row will soon be reached.

REFRESHMENTS:
*The Devonport Hotel,* Middleton-in-Teesdale (tel no: 0325 332255).

# Walk 45     WOLSINGHAM AND TUNSTALL     6m (9.5km)

Maps: OS Sheets Landranger 92 & 87; Outdoor Leisure 31.

*A strenuous walk from the valley bottom to the moors. The wildlife is interesting, the views very good indeed.*

Start: Demesne Mill Picnic Area.

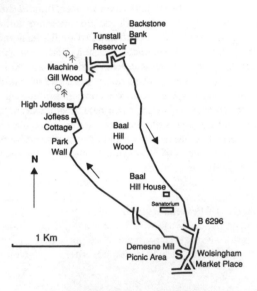

Leave the Picnic Area, near Wolsingham Market Place, through a kissing gate in the north west corner, and follow the path running parallel to Waskerley Beck on your right. Cross a pasture and pass a mill race which once carried water to a mill wheel. Cross a stile and go over the footbridge ahead. Turn left along a hedge. The way is clearly defined by a stone kerb, overgrown for much of its length, indicating that at one time this route was frequently used. The hedge growing on a mound probably marked the boundary of the Bishop's Hunting Park. Go through a kissing gate, and cross a road to another kissing gate. Continue along the Park wall, passing a row of magnificent trees, mainly oak but with some beech, ash, chestnut and pine. Go through a gate – the house on the left is Fawnlees Hall, most of which is protected because of its fine architecture. Continue north-westerly, through gates and edging coniferous plantations to reach moorland over a stile in a high stone wall. From here the retrospective views down to Weardale are very good, and the Cleveland Hills can be seen on the skyline.

Soon the path passes an abandoned farm, Park Wall, on the left, and the ruinous Moorcock Hall. Cross a stile at Park Wall and go right. Go through the left-hand of two gates and continue along a path, then a farm track, to reach Jopless Cottage.

Continue to High Jopless, a large farm. Go through the gate near the farmyard and along the farm road. Turn left on to a field track to reach Tunstall Cottage. Continue along the road to the lodge gates. Turn right and cross the reservoir dam. Continue along a path that zig-zags through **Blackstone Bank Wood**, and at the top of the hill go right along a track. Cross a culvert to the high side of Fawn Wood and bear right where the track splits, going over fields to cross Spring Gill Beck. Follow the path through the middle of three pastures, using six access gates. The sixth gate leads to **Baal Hill Farm**: bear left opposite the farmhouse and continue along a track close to a hedge on your left. On reaching a tarmac road at a kissing gate, turn right, briefly, then left, through another kissing gate. Continue along a path and go through two more kissing gates to reach Wolsingham's Uppertown. Turn right to the Picnic Area.

POINTS OF INTEREST:
**Blackstone Bank Wood** – A rare wood in that it is natural and almost unaffected by man. Sessile oak has been growing here since the Ice Age. Subsequent owners have allowed it to remain as it was for the benefit of the chase.
**Baal Hill Farm** – An ancient house with a 16th century vaulted basement. Clearly seen is the conical roof of the gin-gan where horses drove the farm machinery. Baal Hill, Bole Hill and similar names indicate a place where lead smelting was carried out.

REFRESHMENTS:
Hotels, and pubs in Wolsingham.

Walk 46    **HIGH AND LOW CONISCLIFFE**    6¼m (10km)
Maps: OS Sheets Landranger 93; Pathfinder NZ 21/31.
*A flat riverside walk.*
Start: A lay-by west of Baydale Beck Inn.

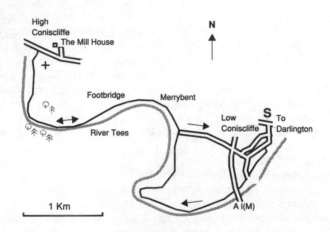

From the lay-by cross the road and go left to a footpath sign. Go right over a stile and along a path to Low Coniscliffe, entering it along a short lane. Continue through the village to Durmast House. There go left along a track to the river. Go right, upstream, along the river bank under a bridge which carries the A1(M) across the River Tees. The walk hugs the river all the way to High Coniscliffe and is filled with interest. Upstream of the motorway bridge the riverbank is regularly used by club anglers fishing for dace and roach. Game fishermen also fish this stretch, standing in the water. The fish they seek are trout and salmon. Several species of tree grow along this riverside, giving shade and binding the bank; sycamore, elm, ash provide the shade, willows lining the water's edge help to prevent erosion while elder, hazel and hawthorn grow beneath the taller trees if there is not too much shade. At the upstream end of this wooded area, where blackthorn grow, note the track leading away on your right because the return journey takes it. The large embankment seen on the south side of the river half-way to High Coniscliffe is a natural feature. The river has swept away the Durham side of it but left the Yorkshire side at its original height. Sand, silt and gravel deposited by the river as it slows and loses its carrying power are what form the basis of the flat fields on the Durham side of the river.

Soon after leaving the shelter of the trees the path passes a stone jetty-like construction in the river. It was built by landlords anxious to prevent erosion of their fields. The south side of Merrybent, with its large houses and extensive gardens is clearly seen from the path. Upstream of Ulnaby Beck, beyond a plantation of larch and pine, the landscape changes – flood plains, terraces, islands and former courses of the river remain as they were originally formed. The path reaches **High Coniscliffe** with its fine church, St Edwins, prominently sited on a limestone outcrop. Having explored the village and sampled the local brew, there is a choice of return routes: go along the roadside footpath and through Merrybent, which is easy, but does little to in spire or, much more interestingly, go back along the riverbank as far as the blackthorn thicket. There go left across fields and along a track to bridge the motorway en route to Low Coniscliffe. From there take the first left, then go left again, back to the lay-by.

POINTS OF INTEREST:

**High Coniscliffe** – The Saxon name for Coniscliffe was CININGSCLIFFE which means Kingscliffe. Edwin of Northumbria was the king and it is to him that High Coniscliffe church is dedicated, the only church in England dedicated to St Edwin. The present church is 13th century but it incorporates Saxon stonework and a Norman door.

REFRESHMENTS:

*The Duke of Wellington,* High Coniscliffe (tel no: 0325 374283).
*The Spotted Dog,* High Coniscliffe (tel no: 0325 374351).
*The Baydale Beck Inn,* Near Low Coniscliffe (tel no: 0325 469637).

# Walk 47     COCKFIELD FELL     6¹/₄m (10km)

Maps: OS Sheets Landranger 92; Pathfinder NZ 12/13.

*An interesting walk through a landscape littered with ancient and industrial history. It is also a good map reading exercise.*

Start: St Mary's Church, Cockfield.

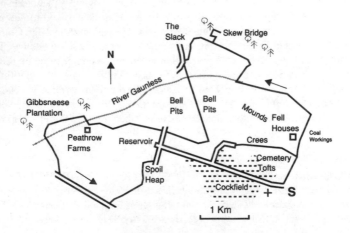

From the church at the eastern end of Cockfield take the path north-easterly to Fell Houses crossing, en route, the dyke, an exhausted quarry from which volcanic dolerite, a green Whinstone, was extracted. Beyond Fell Houses follow the old tramway that was built to carry coal to the Haggerleases Railway, an extension of the Stockton and Darlington Railway. On reaching the disused line where it spanned the River Gaunless on a viaduct, the square stones used to reinforce the opposite riverbank are clearly seen. They were once used as sleepers for the Stockton and Darlington, stone being cheaper than timber. Climb on to the embankment from where, to the left, there are good views of Butterknowle and Copley. The saucer-shaped depressions to the right are old bell pits from which coal was mined. The crows-feet mounds to your left are dumped waste from the dolerite: their shapes are the result of using pulleys, horses and rope-hauled barrows along the waste heaps. Continue along the disused line for $^1/_2$ mile, then turn sharp right on to a well-defined tramway towards the river, passing, on your right, the ditch and mound of a pre-Roman settlement.

Stay on the tramway all the way to the river, and there turn left to reach a sewage works. Here a short diversion, right, to George Dixon's skew-arched bridge is well worth the effort. Returning to the track, continue past the Slack and Haggerleases Station, the line's terminus and go uphill along a track to Cockfield, heading for the abutments of an old railway bridge and up the hill to a group of well-defined bell pits. Continue along an old cart track towards Cockfield, and on reaching a stile turn right over it. Pass a sandstone quarry and go across the site of Holy Moor and Wigglesworth Collieries, and the coke works which coked the coal from New Copley. The route is to the right of Peathrow Farm which is white-washed every year in compliance with a Raby Estates tenancy agreement. Continue across a bridge to Shotton Moor. Soon a surfaced road is reached: go left along it for $^1/_3$ mile to the first stile on the left. Go over and follow a waymarked path to join the road to Cockfield near Holy Moor Farm. Turn left to Bleak Terrace. Pass some pigeon crees and return to the Fell through a wicket gate. Continue to the village boundary wall. Stay on the path, with the wall on our right, to return to the start at St Mary's Church.

POINTS OF INTEREST:
The 600 acres of heavily exploited Cockfield Fell were not included in the 18th century Enclosure Acts and remain today in the tenure of the people of Cockfield. It is common land in the true sense of the word. The rights and customs which the commoners enjoyed 500 years ago are still observed. Several people keep sheep, cattle and horses on this common land and Fell Reeves are still appointed to prevent abuses.

REFRESHMENTS:
Pubs in Cockfield.

# Walk 48    WINSTON AND OLD RICHMOND    6¹/₂m (10km)

Maps: OS Sheets Landranger 92; Pathfinder NZ 01/11.

*An interesting little expedition to see the ruins of Old Richmond.*
Start: At 147171, a short cul-de-sac formed from a piece of the old pre-straightened A67 to the east of Winston.

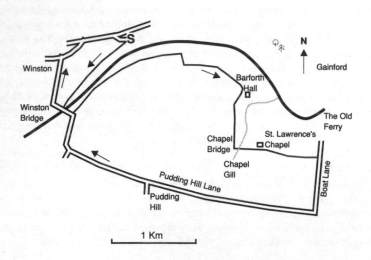

From the eastern end of this section of old road cross a stile into a field and follow a defined path down to the River Tees. Continue upstream, parallel to the river on your left, and keeping to the higher ground to avoid some rather boggy patches close to the riverside. Soon, the splendid Winston Bridge is reached. Cross and turn left over a stile into a field. Walk downstream, edging the river, to some cottages where a bridleway is joined. Follow this clear track, crossing a stone bridge and keeping to the left of a field. After about 1 mile the bridleway makes a sharp right turn, away from the river. Stay with it until it reaches a field gate on the left. Go through this and walk ahead, close to a hedge on the right, until the cottages at Barforth Hall are reached. Go to the left of the cottages and farm buildings – the Hall can be seen to the left – and continue, climbing steadily, close to Chapel Gill on your left. Soon you will make a sharp left turn over Chapel Bridge. A close inspection of the bridge reveals that its architecture is ecclesiastical: this is hardly surprising since by continuing along the clear track the grassy mounds, and the lines of the walls and houses of Old Richmond are much in evidence. Once it was a place of some importance, but it fell on hard times, was abandoned, much of the stonework being removed for field wall building. The ruins of a tiny 13th century chapel, St Lawrence's, and a tower shaped dovecote remain.

Continue along an elevated track, from where there are some fine views northwards, across the roofs of the pre-Norman Conquest village of **Gainford**, nestling snugly on an inside bend of the River Tees. On reaching narrow **Boat Lane** turn right, along it, to reach a T-junction with Pudding Hill Lane. Turn right, soon passing, on your left, Pudding Hill from which the lane gets its name. There is a small reservoir on top of this quaintly named hill. Continue along this quiet lane, passing the lane end to Ovington on the left and continue right, downhill, to re-cross Winston Bridge. Continue up the road and go through the village, bearing right to leave it on to the A67. Here turn right for a short distance, back to the cul-de-sac. An alternative ending, having re-crossed Winston Bridge, is to retrace your steps along the riverside.

## POINTS OF INTEREST:
**Gainford** – The village church succeeds one built in the 9th century by Ecgred, Bishop of Lindisfarne. Gainford Hall is Jacobean, a much more modern structure.
**Boat Lane** – So named because in bygone days there was a regular ferry service operating from its northern end, over the River Tees to Gainford on the opposite bank.

## REFRESHMENTS:
*The Bridgewater Arms,* Winston (tel no: 0325 730302).

Walk 49          THE CONISCLIFFES          6¹/₂m (10km)
Maps: OS Sheets Landranger 93; Pathfinder NZ 21/31.
*A pleasant walk, partly along the River Tees.*
Start: At 253141, the Baydale Beck Inn car park.

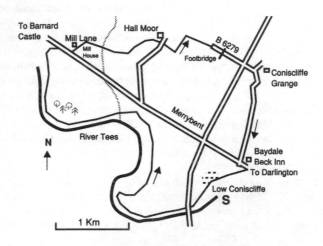

From the car park cross the A67 to a waymarked stile. Cross and go diagonally across
the field ahead to enter Low Coniscliffe, seen ahead, along a short passage. Turn left
along the tarmac road through the village and, where it bifurcates, go left, to reach the
nearby River Tees. Go right, under a bridge that carries a motorway, using a riverside
path. With the River Tees as your guide go upstream along its bank until High
Coniscliffe is reached. There, climb a steep hill to enter the village, mid-way along it,
through a kissing gate close to the **church of St Edwin**. Cross the A67, turn right and
walk eastwards towards the Spotted Dog Inn. Beyond the inn turn left and go along
Mill Lane to Mill House at its end. Go through a field gate on your right into a large
field. Cross nearby Ulnaby Beck on a footbridge and continue diagonally right across
the field to a corner at the end of a stone wall where there are some railings. Cross and
go over the field ahead, then alongside a short hedge on your left. Go across two

narrow fields and keeping in the same direction (eastwards), with a new hedge on your left, cross two fields to enter another over a stile. Turn left for 50 yards to where a green strip, left unploughed because it is a well-preserved right of way, crosses the field. Go along this strip to reach Lark Lane and turn left along it for 50 yards. Turn right through a gateway and take the cart track ahead into the next field. Here a path leads first left, then right. Follow the path along a hedge on your left until a farm road is reached. Stay on this road, crossing the motorway, as far as a T-junction. Turn right along a farm road for 1 mile to reach the A67. Turn left to reach the Baydale Beck Inn, seen ahead, and the end of a very pleasant walk.

POINTS OF INTEREST:
**The Church of St Edwin** – The village church of High Coniscliffe is the only one in England dedicated to this Christian King of Northumbria who was killed in 633 AD.

REFRESHMENTS:
*The Baydale Beck,* Low Coniscliffe (tel no: 0325 469637).
*The Spotted Dog,* Beefeater Steak House, High Coniscliffe (tel no: 0325 74351).
*The Duke of Wellington,* High Coniscliffe (tel no: 0325 74283).

Walk 50          FOREST TEESDALE          6¹/₂m (10km)
Maps: OS Sheets Landranger 92; Outdoor Leisure 31.
*Lovely riverside scenery and panoramic views across Upper Teesdale and Ettergill Valley are highlights of this delightful walk.*
Start: At 885286, the High Force Hotel car park.

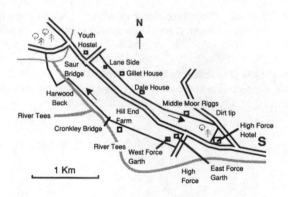

From the Hotel turn right along the B6277, Middleton-in-Teesdale to Alston road. After ¹/₄ mile, turn left along a quarry road for 300 yards and then turn right, through a gate, on to a clear bridleway. Follow it, passing two farms on your right, East Force Garth and West Force Garth. Resist the temptation to stay on the bridleway, which leads to a quarry: just past another farm, Force Garth End, where the bridleway curves to the right, go left, briefly, to a wall and turn right, along it. Keep close to the wall, on your left, to reach a facing field gate nicely sited for leaning on to savour the delights of Widdybank Fell and Cronkley Fell, between which the clear waters of the infant Tees thread so agreeably. Go through the gate and continue straight ahead to a farm road. Turn left along it, downhill, to Cronkley Bridge, where there is a brief encounter with the Pennine Way. Keeping on the river's left bank, go upstream, passing the confluence of Harwood Beck and the Tees, and continuing with only Harwood Beck for company. When you reach Saur Bridge cross and turn right, leaving the Pennine Way. Keeping close to the river, continue upstream to where Langdon Beck spills in on the far side and there, at a farm, cross Harwood Beck on a concrete bridge and turn right along a surfaced road to Langdon Beck Hotel. From the hotel rejoin the nearby B6277 and turn right along it for $3/_4$ mile. Just beyond a Youth Hostel, turn left along a farm road leading to East Under Hurth Farm. At the end of the first field turn right, through a gate, and continue close to a wall on your right, passing Lane Side Farm. On approaching the next farm, Gillet House, cross to the other side of the wall, thus keeping to the right of way. Go down a narrow enclosure to Forest School, passing behind this building and going on to Dale House Farm. The way ahead is now along a sunken track as far as Dale Cottage. From there it is along a metalled road to Middle Moor Riggs, the next farm. Continue along a broad, green, sunken track from where the sweeping views of Ettergill Valley, on your left, are particularly good. When a surfaced road is reached at Dirt Pit (see Note to Walk 80). Cross a stile on your right into a field. Cross diagonally left to a stile in a wall. Cross to complete the last few steps of the walk.

## POINTS OF INTEREST:

Much of the second half of this walk is along the route of the original main road, from Langdon Beck to Newbiggin via Dirt Pit, which was in regular use until the B6277 was built circa 1820.

## REFRESHMENTS:

*The Langdon Beck Hotel*  (tel no: 0833 22267).
*The High Force Hotel*  (tel no: 0833 22264).

Walk 51    CROFT TO MIDDLETON-ONE-ROW    6¹/₂m (10km)
Maps: OS Sheets Landranger 93; Pathfinder NZ 20/30 & 21/31.
*An easy walk of varied character.*
Start: At 289099, St Peter's Church, Croft.
Finish: Middleton-One-Row.

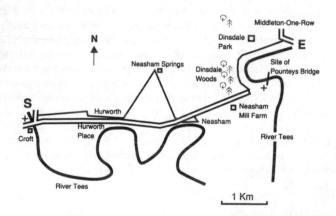

From St Peter's Church cross the **River Tees**, using the road bridge, and follow the road as it bends left, passing a 'Land of the Prince Bishops' sign. On leaving the village, just past the Lodge, turn right over a stile and continue along the field edge to an embankment. At its top veer diagonally left and cross another stile. Continue uphill and cross the railway line by footbridge. Go straight ahead on a clear path to Hurworth, crossing stiles. At an old tree the path leaves fields and widens into a track between a wall and a fence, which leads to Roundhill Road. Turn right, then left, into Hurworth Green. Continue eastwards across the Green, passing a plaque to William Emerson, Mathematician. Once across the green, turn left at the Otter & Fish, and at the end of the terrace of houses on Strait Lane turn right along a track past Pear Tree Cottage.

    At the end of the track turn left through a waymarked gate. Pass a farm on your right, enter the field ahead and cross it to a stile. Now bear left for a short distance and cross a footbridge. Bear right across a field and exit over another stile. Go diagonally across the next field and exit at a corner stile. Go left to a minor road. Cross and continue as indicated by a footpath sign to a telegraph post, where a waymarker directs you to a waymarked stile. Descend diagonally to another stile. Cross and go along the right edge of the next field to cross a footbridge and stile. Go along the left-hand side of the next field to join a bridleway just south of Neasham Springs Farm. Go right along this into Neasham. Cross the main road, bear left to the riverside embankment and turn left along it to Stockburn Lane. Turn left back into Neasham. At a crossroads go right, uphill, and continue past Neasham Hill Farm. Half a mile beyond the farm turn left at a creeper-covered tree and take the wide, signposted path for 100 yards. Cross a stile on the right and descend a field close to a hedge on the left to reach a waymarked stile near an electricity pole. Cross the field ahead diagonally, crossing a footbridge over a beck, and continue to St John's parish Church at Low Dinsdale. Across from the church stands the old Rectory with its horse mounting block. Return to the bridge through a kissing gate and go diagonally right across the field to reach Dinsdale Wood over a stile. Where the path splits go right, towards the river, and continue to a brick footbridge. Here turn sharp right, uphill, and continue along a clear path, crossing a second brick footbridge. When a house, Dinsdale Spa, comes into view, take the left-hand path, going to the right of the building. From the Spa car park continue along the riverbank, and where the path forks beneath a large brick house, go left, uphill, into picturesque Middleton-One-Row.

## POINTS OF INTEREST:

**River Tees** – The southern boundary of the ancient County Palatine of Durham was marked by the River Tees which the Prince Bishops ruled as though it were a different country. The walk visits three different crossing points into the county that were all used in the days of the Prince Bishops.

## REFRESHMENTS:

*The Comet*, Hurworth (tel no: 0325 721268).
*The Bay Horse*, Hurworth (tel no: 0325 720663).
*The Otter & Fish*, Hurworth (tel no: 0325 720019).
*The Fox & Hounds*, Neasham (tel no: 0325 720350).

Walk 52          **CASTLE EDEN DENE**          7m (11km)
Maps: OS Sheets Landranger 88 and 93; Pathfinder NZ 44 and
NZ 43/53.
*A walk through one of the largest woodlands of the North-East
which has not been either planted or extensively altered by man.*
Start: Oakerside Dene Lodge.

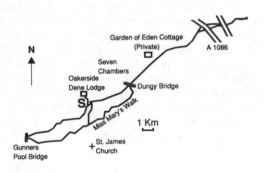

The directions are given from Oakerside Dene Lodge, but there are six more entrances
to the **Castle Eden Dene Nature Reserve**.

From the Lodge enter the Dene and at a T-junction of paths turn left and, ignoring
a path going right, continue between Seven Chambers on your left and Castle Eden
Burn on your right. The Dene is a steep sided valley that was cut into the magnesium
limestone of East Durham by glacial meltwaters. Subsequent glacial activity covered
it and the surrounding plateau with a thick layer of boulder clay. The clay slopes of
the Dene are unstable and there are frequent landslips. In certain areas the underlying
limestone is exposed, often as cliffs, as at Seven Chambers. As you follow the path
downstream, crossing it on a footbridge and, a little further on, re-crossing it, you are

walking through acres of dense woodland. The steepest slopes of the Dene, particularly the central part, are clothed in oak, Wych elm and yew. This yew-rich woodland is a feature unique in the North of England.

On re-crossing to the burn's northern bank continue along what is the only path in this part of the Dene. When a branch right is reached, ignore it and keep on to where the path splits just short of the A1086. Take either branch and go under the road. The branches re-continue before going under a railway bridge. The next turn to the right leads out of the Dene on to a road leading to the A1086. Here you should begin to retrace your steps. The character of the Dene at its eastern, Denemouth, end is gentler than further upstream. The valley floor is broader, the slopes less steep. Here the woodland is not as varied, being mainly sycamore scrub. Retrace your steps to the footbridge over the burn, passing on your left a side path which leads to the Dene's edge. The shrubs seen throughout the walk include hawthorn, blackthorn, wild rose, alder, hazel, and holly. The woodland also supports most of the more common breeding birds along with Green and Greater spotted woodpeckers and nuthatches. Once over the bridge, an interesting detour left leads to the Dene's edge and along Miss Mary's Walk to an exit at the site of a castle. Otherwise retrace your steps almost to where you started and go left to cross the burn and continue through the woods, keeping just inside them and, ignoring a path gong right, continue to re-cross the burn on Gunner's Pool Bridge. Beyond, take the first path to the right to return to Oakerside Dene Lodge.

POINTS OF INTEREST:
**Castle Eden National Natural Reserve** – Like an oasis in a desert. Rare, nationally endangered species of flies and beetles live here in a highly specialised habitat.

REFRESHMENTS:
None in the Dene, but there are hotels, pubs and cafés in Peterlee.

Maps: OS Sheets Landranger 92; Outdoor Leisure 30.

*A very beautiful walk through a gill immortalised by Sir Walter Scott.*

Start: At 071123, the village of Brignall.

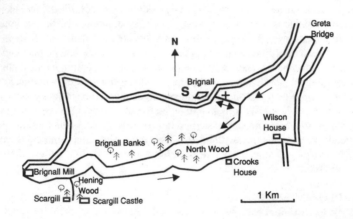

Leave Brignall through a field gate between the church and some farm buildings. Go straight ahead for 100 yards, turn right over a little bridge into a second field and then left to join a green track. Follow the track down a shallow gill to join a footpath and turn right along it, passing, on your left, the ruins of St Mary's church, which was abandoned in 1833 when the new village church was consecrated. The path leads into a wood where it goes half right. Leave the wood at its top corner through a railed fence to enter a second wood. Continue along the well-defined path through a deep glen, close to the River Greta which is on your left and sometimes 100 feet below you. At Brignall Mill – at the end of the **Brignall Banks** – cross the River Greta on a footbridge and continue uphill, still on the defined path, for a few yards before turning left for the return journey along the stream's south bank, following a clearly defined, undulating, green track. Where this track bifurcates, go left to the river and continue along its bank for a short distance to reach a footbridge over a feeder. Before crossing, a detour can be made up the side gill, with the feeder on your right, to Scargill Castle, an old pele-tower. Back at the River Greta continue downstream, still on a well-defined path, to a second feeder. Cross this close to its confluence with the Greta. Climb through bracken to a field on the hill top and turn left. Keeping within the wood, continue along the top of the bank close to a fence on your right: because parts of the path are somewhat overgrown, brief detours into the adjoining field are helpful, through strictly not the thing to do. On leaving the wood, continue past the rear of Crooks House to join a farm road which passes Wilson House, on its left, when it reaches the Barningham-Greta Bridge road. Go straight ahead, along the road which soon turns left. After $^1/_2$ mile go over a stile on your left and go downhill, across scrub, to a stile in a stone wall. Cross this, and the field ahead to reach Greta Bridge, the very lovely bow-bridge. Cross the bridge. At a footpath sign ahead, turn left over a stile in a wall and go half-right, uphill, and continue close to a fence on your right to cross a facing stile. Stay close to a fence on your right to cross a facing stile. Stay close to a fence and plantation on your left, at the end of which cross a stile in the corner of the wire fence ahead. Go diagonally left, down a field, cross a shallow gill and, at a second one – the one used on the outward journey – turn right, up it, and retrace your steps to Brignall village.

## POINTS OF INTEREST:
**Brignall Banks** – Sir Walter Scott rhapsodised eloquently about the Banks:-

> *'O Brignall Banks are wild and fair*
> *And Greta's woods are green*
> *And you may gather garlands there,*
> *Would grace a summer queen'.*

## REFRESHMENTS:
*The Morritt Arms Hotel,* Greta Bridge (tel no: 0833 27232).

# Walk 54    BARNARD CASTLE AND BOLDRON    7m (11km)

Maps: OS Sheets Landranger 92; Outdoor Leisure 31.

*Part of this pleasant walk is along an almost forgotten footpath.*

Start: The Barnard Castle Butter Market.

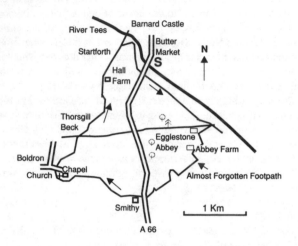

From the Butter Market go downhill, along the A67, and where it turns right continue straight ahead to cross the River Tees on a footbridge. Turn left along a riverside path past some houses on your right. Keep on the path, which soon bears right, away from the river, to join a bridlepath over a stile. Turn right and go through a caravan park, uphill. About half way through the park, cross a stile on your left to go over the hill's brow to a handgate. From here there are good views of Bowes Museum and the roof tops of Barnard Castle. Follow the hedge on your left to reach a minor road and go left along it, with the Tees on your left for company, passing an old packhorse bridge. When the approach road to Egglestone Abbey (see Note to Walk 9) is reached, turn right along it if you wish to visit these interesting ruins before continuing towards Abbey Farm. On approaching the farm, take the first turn on your left and immediately after passing the last building, turn left again to go through a field gate. Now turn right and continue alongside the hedge on your right to another field gate. Go through, turn left and go around two sides of the field to a corner stile. Cross and, keeping parallel to a plantation on your right, go ahead across a field. At its bottom corner go through a field gate on your left and continue close to the fence on your right for 300 yards to where there is a large boulder at each side of the fence. These mark the site of an old stile. Cross near the boulders and follow the hedge on your right. Go through the gate ahead and, with Castle Farm on your right, go diagonally across the next two fields to the smithy at Cross Lanes. Go through a field gate behind the smithy and continue, keeping close to a hedge, for two fields. Cross a stile on your left and immediately go right, close to the hedge on your right, to the next stile. Cross and continue along the fence on your left to another stile. Cross this and other stiled fields ahead into Boldron.

Turn right at the village green between a chapel and a church and cross a stile near a house. Go down the centre of a field to a second stile. Cross and go half right to a stile and, keeping in the same direction over the fields, cross two more stiles and Thorsgill Beck on a stone footbridge. Go right for a few yards. Cross a fence to the next field and go half left uphill, and through a gateway. Walk parallel to the road ahead, keeping close to the hedge on your left, until you are just past Hall Farm. There join the road over a stile on your left. Go right, along the road. Turn left for a few yards at a junction and cross a stile in the stone wall ahead. Follow a hedge leading to a field, then go along a clear path to the County Bridge over the Tees. Cross the bridge and follow a road, at first beside the river, then going left and uphill, back to the Butter Market.

REFRESHMENTS:
There are hotels, pubs and cafés in Barnard Castle.

## Walk 55  BARNARD CASTLE, FLATTS WOOD AND COTHERSTONE

7m (11km)

Maps: OS Sheets Landranger 92; Outdoor Leisure 31.

*A delight at any time of the year.*

Start: The bottom, west, end of Galgate, Barnard Castle.

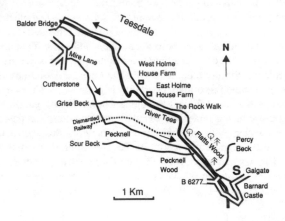

Leave Barnard Castle (see Note to Walk 36) between the Post Office and the Methodist Chapel to Scar Top where a 'To the Woods' sign directs you down to Flatts Wood. Staying on the west bank of the River Tees, follow the path upstream, crossing Percy Beck on a footbridge. Follow the path for 1 mile to where it bifurcates, and take the lower path, descending steeply through pleasantly wooded riverside scenery. Go upstream past the remains of the demolished Tees Valley viaduct. Climb steadily and ignoring a track on the right, descend to the riverside along the popular **Rock Walk**, passing between two large, moss-covered rocks (the **Wishing Stones**). The way ahead is along the water's edge, below over hanging cliffs. Beyond these climb a stone staircase, 29 steps high, to re-enter the wood, and turn left along a riverside path. Ignoring any tracks to the right, stay with this path for $^1/_2$ mile and leave the wood through a waymarked gate into a large pasture. Keeping close to the wood on our right, go straight ahead for 100 yards, then turn right through a waymarked gate back into the wood for a steep climb up to a stile leading to fields. Go left along the woodside edge of the first field and from the second, in front of East Holme House Farm on our right, follow waymarkers past West Holme House Farm, seen ahead. Beyond this farm cross two waymarked fields and from the third one cross a stile on your left to descend a path and cross a gill on a stone footbridge. Go uphill and through a gate in a facing wall. Cross the next field towards another gate, but do not go through it. Instead, turn right and follow the wall on your left for three fields. Cross a wall stile and follow a pleasant path along a wooded bank to an equally pleasant pasture. Now cross the River Tees on the bridge seen ahead, turn left, cross a feeder (the Baler) and climb the tarmac path to the B6277. Turn left into Cotherstone (see Note to Walk 1). Beyond Meadowcroft turn left again into Mire Lane. Go along this to a field. Cross to a corner stile in a short wall on your right. Go along the side of the next field to a waymarked stile near a holly bush. Cross and go right, over the next field. Cross another waymarked stile in a facing fence. Bear half left, cross to the corner of Grise Beck Wood and go over a farm bridge to the right of it. At the end of the field turn right at a gate and follow a path over a disused railway. Still heading in the same direction, cross the next field, go under another disused railway and cross another field to exit through a gate on to a track. Turn left, go through a gate, past a cottage and along a field path to Peckwith Farm. Beyond the farm go behind an isolated house and follow yellow arrows into Peckwith Wood. Soon you join a bridleway: follow it for $^1/_2$ mile to reach the B6277. Turn left, cross the Tees and retrace your steps to the start.

## POINTS OF INTEREST:
**Rock Walk** – This popular walk was created more than 100 years ago by Dr George Edwards who first had to get permission from the Earl of Darlington. It is one of three well known walks in Flatts Wood.

**Wishing Stones** – If you pass between these two rocks without touching them your wish will be granted.

## REFRESHMENTS:
There are several hotels, pubs and cafés in Barnard Castle.
*The Fox and Hounds,* Cotherstone (tel no: 0833 50241).
*The Red Lion,* Cotherstone (tel no: 0833 50236).

# Walk 56   BARNARD CASTLE AND LARTINGTON     7m (11km)

Maps: OS Sheets Landranger 92; Outdoor Leisure 31.

*An excellent walk, but see below.*

Start: Galgate, Barnard Castle.

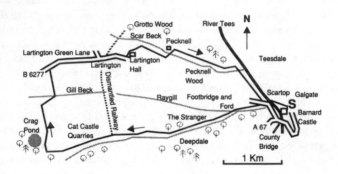

Because the first third of this walk, through Deepdale Wood, is along beck-side paths that have suffered from erosion in parts and since there are some fallen trees to negotiate, this walk is more suited to the hardy walker than the casual stroller.

Leave the bottom end of Galgate going between the Post Office and the Methodist Church to Scar Top Park. Follow the path signposted 'To the Woods' through Flatts Wood and down to the River Tees. Cross on a bridge called Deepdale Aqueduct to reach the B6277. Cross the road to enter Deepdale, a delightful deciduous wood, through a gate. Take the track along Deepdale Beck on your left for $^1/_2$ mile to Ray Gill. Either ford or cross on a nearby footbridge to rejoin the track. Continue westwards to where a wooden footbridge crosses the beck, descend to water level, but remain on the beck's northern bank. Keep going upstream, scrambling over rocks and exposed tree roots for about 30 feet to rejoin the main path. After a further $^1/_2$ mile, where Smart

Gill joins Deepdale Beck from the south and just past a large uprooted tree on your left, there is a moss covered boulder of Shap granite called **The Stranger**. This is where the real fun begins because just upstream of this the path has slipped into the beck. The best way around is by holding on to the branches and exposed roots of handy trees. Once past this little difficulty, rejoin the path at stream level. Soon, when the path bifurcates, take the right-hand fork, uphill. The left hand path drops towards the beck and becomes impassable because of the felled and fallen trees lying across it. The right-hand one will take you to the buttress ends of demolished Deepdale Viaduct, beyond which you pass, on our right, **Cat Castle Quarries**. Continue along the path into a wood as far as a wall. There go along an escarpment to a farm road near the private Crag Pond. Now turn right, northwards, along a gated bridleway for 1 mile to Lartington Green Lane. Turn right for 1 mile of unavoidable road walking into Lartington. Go through the village and just beyond 'Yew Trees' turn left along a carriageway. Turn right opposite the cemetery as indicated by a 'Barnard Castle' fingerpost, go along a path, through a copse and over a stile into Lartington Hall Park. Passing Lartington Hall – built during the reign of Charles I – on your right, go diagonally half left across a field and cross a huge ladder stile. Continue along a path, eastwards, near Scar Beck and leave the park through a gate. Turn left along a cart road to pass Pecknell Grange Farm on your left before turning right through a gate. Keep going eastward, following yellow arrows and passing behind Pecknell Cottage. On reaching Pecknell Wood go through it and turn right along a cart road back to the B6277. From there return to Galgate along the outward route.

POINTS OF INTEREST:
**The Stranger** – This chunk of pink granite is better known locally as The Great Stone or The Boulder Stone. Deposited by a glacier 10,000 years ago, it weighs almost 30 tons.
**Cat Castle Quarries** – So named because at one time there was a castle in this vicinity in which lived a family of wild cats.

REFRESHMENTS:
There are hotels, pubs and cafés in Barnard Castle.

## Walk 57  MIDDLETON-IN-TEESDALE AND HARDBERRY HILL  7m (11km)

Maps: OS Sheets Landranger 92; Outdoor Leisure 31.

*Magnificent views compensate for the uphill work on this very enjoyable walk.*

Start: The car park, Middleton-in-Teesdale.

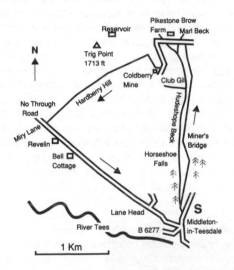

**Caution:** Do not explore the old lead mines: the shaft levels are unsafe.

From the car park go left past the Bainbridge Memorial Fountain, cross Bridge Street and go along the Market Place on the B6277. Where this bends left, continue ahead past a church on your right and the remains of stocks on your left, going steeply uphill. Where a former quarry road, Beck Road, branches left through woods turn left along it, northwards, for a mile. Then, just before the road bridges Hudeshope Beck, take a track, right, past Skears Lime Kilns. Where the track bifurcates to skirt a high mound, the choice of routes is yours, because both paths rejoin at the far side to climb a steep bank and enter lovely Snaisgill Plantation. Weaving delightfully through trees high above Hudeshope Beck, the track leaves the wood over a ladder stile into a field.

122

Continue northwards close to a stone wall on your left, crossing stiles. Go over a pasture to join a track as it goes through a wooden gate: Go through the gate and downhill towards the pleasant Hudeshope Beck, going through an open area of grassland, sprinkled with bushes and green spoil heaps which rabbits have warrened. The way ahead is along a grass track, short cropped and edged with a sprinkling of larches. The track crosses a horizontal mine tunnel close to a stone building and continues through an open gateway to cross Marl Beck. The beck is fairly wide and there is no bridge, so after a period of wet weather it may be necessary to detour upstream until a safe crossing is found. On the far bank cross a stile in the wall ahead and go over a stretch of rough pasture, walking due north, to join an un-enclosed road which crosses your line of walk at right angles. Turn left along the road, crossing Hudeshope Beck on a bridge, and bending left. Just before a defunct, grass-covered reservoir on your right, turn right along a track, passing a brick building and a shaft level. Turn left and continue in front of a mine shop, near the level mouth of **Coldberry Mine**, opposite. Continue through the mine workings along the right side of double walls, climbing and aiming for a pair of chimney pots. Continue past a water trough. The way ahead is now undefined: continue to a gate in the corner of a rough pasture. Climb over it – it is too securely fastened to open – and continue half right across a pasture to a stile in a wire fence. Cross and aim for the corner of a field where there are three gates: go through the rusty, middle one. Follow a path over four fields to join a rutted track. Continue along it and go steeply downhill to join quiet Middleside road close to Revelin Farm. Turn left along this high level road for two very enjoyable miles back to Middleton (see Note to Walk 5) and the start of the walk.

POINTS OF INTEREST:
**Coldberry Mine** – The mine was one of the largest in Teesdale. Lead was mined there for several centuries before it closed in 1955. Many ruins including the mine shop, dams, dressings, levels and shafts.

REFRESHMENTS:
There are several hotels and pubs, and a café, in Middleton-in-Teesdale.

Walk 58    **ROMALDKIRK AND COTHERSTONE**    7m (11km)

Maps: OS Sheets Landranger 92; Outdoor Leisure 31.

*A fairly easy walk along riverside and field paths.*

Start: St Romald's Church, Romaldkirk.

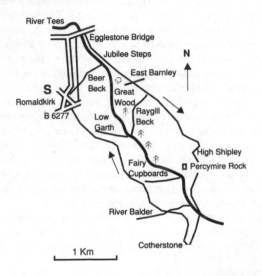

Leave Romaldkirk by the bottom of the village green, going left along a signposted lane to cross Beer Beck on a slab bridge. Turn right to cross a wall stile on your left. Continue along the path ahead, climbing gently over waymarked, stiled pastures to Egglestone Bridge. Turn right to cross the Tees. Go along the B6281 to reach a public footpath sign on the right. Cross a ladder stile here, and take an access road for almost $^1/_4$ mile. At the road end, go left over a stile signposted 'Footpath to East Barnley Farm' and go into Great Wood. Climb a series of 48 steps, the **Jubilee Steps**, edged by railway sleepers, to leave the wood through a gate. Go right, across fields, to pass East Barnley Farm on your right. Now follow a track through a waymarked gate and go left, up a ridge, to the head of Raygill. Cross a stile and go ahead, over another stile, to a farm track. Go left along it to High Shipley – once a hunting lodge of James II. Turn right for a few yards, right again through a gate and go downhill, beside a plantation. Go left to a corner stile and take the path along the valley bottom. Continue through a waymarked gate into a field. Cross the field, go over a beck and, keeping it on your left, go on to a corner gate. There go right along a path beside a wall on your right. When a stile in the wall is reached, go over for a short detour to Percymine Rock, from where there are panoramic views of Teesdale.

Back at the stile, go right, along a path, downhill, and cross a stile on your right into Shipley Wood. Turn left and go out of it over a stile. The way is now downhill to a caravan site. Crossing two more stiles, take the path to the Tees. Cross on a footbridge and turn left for a detour into Cotherstone (see Note to Walk 1). Back at the bridge continue upstream, close to the Tees on your right, to reach a waymarked stile on your left. Go over, turn right and follow a path round a field close to a hedge on your right as far as a stile in it. Cross, turn left and cross nearby Wilden Beck on stepping stones. Cross a walled orchard and Woden Croft Farm, beyond which detour along a cart track and through a gate to the Fairy Cupboards, riverside pot holes and hollows. Retrace your steps down the cart track to where the detour began. Turn right and go diagonally left over a field, past an ancient ruin, and along a path beside a wood to a waymarked gate. Turn right and head for a narrow gate beyond a shallow dip. Go right, through a waymarked gate. Continue past Low Garth Farm on your right and go along a cart track to a gate in the hedge on your right. Now go diagonally over two pastures into Sennings Lane and so back to **Romaldkirk**.

## POINTS OF INTEREST:
**Jubilee Steps** – The steps in Great Wood were constructed in 1985 to mark the 50th anniversary of the Ramblers' Association.
**Romaldkirk** – The village church, which dates from 1155, replaced one destroyed by Norsemen in 1086. It is known as the Cathedral of the Dales.

## REFRESHMENTS:
*The Rose and Crown,* Romaldkirk (tel no: 0833 50603).
*The Fox and Hounds,* Cotherstone (tel no: 0833 50241).
*The Red Lion,* Cotherstone (tel no: 0833 50236).

**LOWER BALDERSDALE**  7m (11km)

Maps: OS Sheets Landranger 92; Outdoor Leisure 31.
*A walk on infrequently used field and moorland paths.*
Start: The village of Cotherstone.

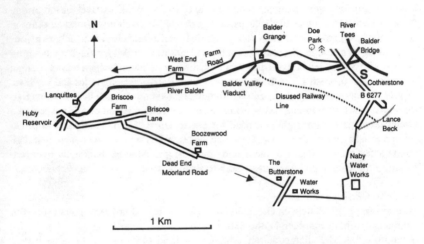

Leave Cotherstone along the B6277, crossing the Balder River. At the north end of Balder Bridge go left through a gate and down some steps. Continue forward, over a stile, then go half right through reeds to a wooded bank. Follow the good path between the trees to the bank top. Turn left along the edge of the field above the trees. Cross a stile near a gate and continue westwards along the edges of four more gated and stiled fields. When the Balder Valley Viaduct is seen to your left, aim for a ladder stile. Cross and go across the middle of a field to the disused Tees Valley Railway line. Cross the line, using ladder stiles at each side of it. Cross the next field and go through a gate in the far bottom corner. Turn left along a farm road for $1/4$ mile to West End Farm. Turn right at the farm, going through the farmyard, then left by a barn. Keep close to a wall on your left and go through a gate in the far field corner. Cross the next field to a wall stile and continue over a rough pasture. Go through a gate near a hawthorn bush, and keep going westwards with a wire fence on your left. When almost across the field bear right towards a large gap in a wall. Cross a small enclosure to a stile partly hidden by a hawthorn bush. Cross and leap a small beck beyond. Scramble up the bank between bushes, turn left through a gap in the corner of a wall and go right, along the wall, to a barn. Cross a stile near a gate and go ahead to reach a wall on your right. Go left along a track, downhill, to a footbridge. Climb out of the weeded valley, and walk forward through a gap, keeping close to the wall. Go through a gate near a barn to reach, just ahead, double gates. Turn left down a track, passing Lanquittes, a holiday cottage, and follow the farm road to Hury Bridge. Cross and go left along Briscoe Lane for $^1/_2$ mile to the lane's end at Booze Wood Farm. Continue along a path signed as a public bridleway (the middle one), bearing half right, (SE), over the moor along a faint trod that soon becomes a clear track, crossing two plank bridges before deteriorating among rough tussocky grass. Keep on until the Bowes-Cotherstone Road is reached, passing **The Butterstone**. Turn right along the road for 150 yards to reach a signed bridlepath on your left. Follow this to Naby Farm and there turn left through a gate with a footpath sign. Follow the farm track northwards to a white gate. Go through and immediately turn right by a hedge, then left along another hedge of the same field. Continue northwards across the next field to a securely tied gate and straddle the fence close to it. Go half left down the middle of the next field, between hawthorn bushes, making for a cart bridge ahead. Do not cross it. Squeeze instead, between the bridge side and a tree and so enter the next field. Go along its left side and through a gate in the corner, close to a holly bush. Cross a concrete ladder-stile into a field. Cross diagonally to reach Cotherstone through a gate. Now pass St Cuthbert's church to reach the main street, the B6277, where the walk began.

## POINTS OF INTEREST:

**The Butterstone** – So called because butter was left on it for people made outcasts because they had fallen victim of the Great Plague of 1636. Money to pay for the butter was placed in jars of vinegar which were left on the stone.

Doe Park, an ancient farmhouse seen a field away to the north from atop the wooded bank close to the start of the walk, was once part of the old hunting preserve belonging to the Lords of Cotherstone Castle.

## REFRESHMENTS:

*The Red Lion*, Cotherstone (tel no: 0833 50236).
*The Fox and Hounds*, Cotherstone (tel no: 0833 50241).

# Walk 60    St John's Chapel and Cowshill    7m (11km)
## Maps: OS Sheets Landranger 87 & 92; Pathfinder NZ 84/94 & Outdoor Leisure 31.

*The more demanding higher, soggy, moorland contrasts nicely with the gentler riverside terrain to give the walk a good balance.*
Start: St John's Chapel village.

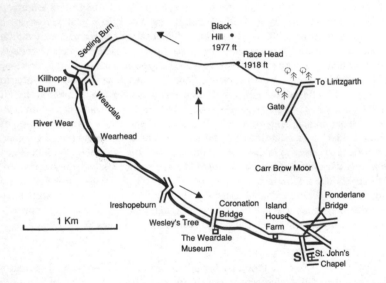

Leave St John's Chapel along the lane behind the Town Hall and, near cottages, turn left over Harthope Burn. Go right at a public footpath sign. Go along the path, over Ponderlane Bridge and straight ahead to some railed steps. Climb these and cross the field ahead. Leave it at a signposted stile on to a road. Cross to a signposted, stiled path. Follow this up two pastures, climbing steeply, to the next road. Turn left. At a bridleway sign turn right, along a walled stony track, climbing steadily for 1 mile across Carr Brow Moor to join the Middlehope Road. Turn right, up the road, and, where it swings right, turn left along a rutted track through a plantation to join the **Wear Valley Way**. Leave the plantation through a gate and continue westwards for $2^1/_2$ miles to Cowshill, climbing steadily initially to cross Race Head, at 1918 feet the highest point on the walk. At the foot of the descent to Cowshill, go through a gate and turn left along a mine road into the village. Leave Cowshill along the lower road, past the Post Office. Opposite Rose Cottage, turn left to cross Burtreeford Bridge, a few yards beyond which go left, through a gate at a footpath sign, to join the **Weardale Way**. Follow the path through a gateway. Go right as far as a corner wall, and there go downhill and continue across stiled pastures alongside Killhope Burn to **Wearhead**. Go through the village, cross Wearhead Bridge and turn left along a signposted path which follows the River Wear's right bank across tiled pastures as far as an intersecting road. Turn left along this road and cross a bridge over the River Wear to reach West Blackdene hamlet. Continue downstream, along the rivers left bank, as far as the second bridge, Coronation Bridge. A diversion over the bridge is recommended to visit the **Weardale Museum and Wesley's Tree**. Having re-crossed Coronation Bridge, continue downstream, passing a waterfall and a ford. Once past Island House Farm, continue eastwards through gated and stiled fields back to Ponderland Bridge. Cross and return to St John's Chapel by the route used n the outward journey.

POINTS OF INTEREST:
**Wear Valley Way** – A 46 mile walk from Killhope Wheel Picnic Area to Willington Picnic Area.
**Weardale Way** – A 78 mile walk along the River Wear from Monkwearmouth to Cowshill.
**Wearhead** – The village is where Killhope Burn and Burnhope Burn join to become the River Wear.
**Weardale Museum and Wesley's Tree** – The Museum contains a Wesley Room and a Weardale Room that is furnished in mid-19th century style. Information on local minerals and the railway line is also on display.
John Wesley visited Weardale several times. On his first visit to Ireshopeburn on 26th May 1752, he preached beside a thorn tree. A commemorative plaque carries the following inscription: Rev John Wesley (1703-1791). Renowned evangelist and founder of Methodism preached in this vicinity on some of his frequent visits to Weardale. Behind is the hawthorn tree, the thorn tree, where he is supposed to have preached.

REFRESHMENTS:
There are several pubs in St John's Chapel.
*The Cowshill Hotel,* Cowshill (tel no: 0388 5372376).

# Walk 61   SUNDERLAND BRIDGE AND SHINCLIFFE   7m (11km)

Maps: OS Sheets Landranger 93 & 88; Pathfinder NZ 23/33 & NZ 24/34.

*A delightful walk, in part along the River Wear.*

Start: At 268377, Sunderland Bridge.

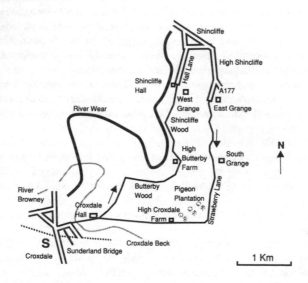

From Sunderland Bridge go into the Croxdale Estate, through readily identifiable entrance gates, and along the carriageway under the A167. Continue down an avenue of sycamore trees, crossing a cattle grid, then Croxdale Beck. Go uphill past **Croxdale Hall**. Turn left to pass a disused, medieval church and face a large stone barn, known locally as 'The Hay Shed'. Between the church and the barn, turn left, then right, up a surfaced lane which edges Croxdale Wood. After $^1/_2$ mile, at Croxdale Wood House, turn right, past Woodhouse Cottage on your right. The way ahead, now unsurfaced, skirts Butterby Wood and brings you, after $^1/_2$ mile, to white-washed High Butterby Farm, on your left. Turn right for a few yards, then left at a yellow waymarker post which directs you into **Shincliffe Wood** along a public footpath. Soon, beyond some tall vegetation, the path becomes steps which descend to the River Wear. At the river, turn right, downstream, along a riverside path via more steps. At the end of the riverside path, where a notice on a tree says 'Durham A C Private Fishing', turn right, away from the Wear, following a path that keeps just within the wood to reach Shincliffe Hall after ¹/₂ mile. Continue ahead, up Hall Lane, for a further ¹/₂ mile to Shincliffe village. Turn right along the tree lined main street to reach the A177. Turn right, using a road side footpath for ¹/₂ mile to High Shincliffe. Take care here because the A177 is a very busy road. At a High Shincliffe bypass road sign, cross to the tarmac lane opposite, Strawberry Lane (an old drovers road), and walk southwards along it. Where it bends right, continue along the unsignposted track ahead and cross a stile close to a gap. Turn left along a field edge to reach a rusty gate. Turn right and follow the path close to another hedge of the same field. At the end of the field go through a gap in the hedge ahead on to an enclosed path and continue southwards along it. To the right the old grandstand of Shincliffe racecourse, now a barn, can be seen. Continue along a stone track to enter an enclosed lane through a narrow gap. Exit over a stile. Keep straight ahead, cross a farm road, and use a wide farm road to reach a stile beside a gate. Cross and maintain the same direction, going through a gate beside Pigeon Plantation, and taking a faint path near a drainage ditch over a field to reach a stile by a gate. Cross an follow the path ahead into some fir trees. When an intersecting path is reached, turn right along it. Cross a plank bridge and go through a gap in the fence near a gate. Continue along the field edge, cross another stile near a gate and take the enclosed path ahead to join a track leading around High Croxdale Farm. Now follow a broad track for ¹/₂ mile to Croxdale and complete the final part of the walk along the outward route.

## POINTS OF INTEREST:
**Croxdale Hall** – The Hall, the seat of the Salvin family, whose home it remains, was built around 1760 by General Salvin. It is not open to the public.
**Shincliffe Wood** – is maintained by the Dean and Chapter of Durham Cathedral.

## REFRESHMENTS:
*The Swan Stars,* Shincliffe (tel no: 09143 848454).

# Walk 62  STAINDROP AND STREATLAM PARK WALL  7m (11km)

Maps: OS Sheets Landranger 92; Pathfinder NZ 12/13 & Outdoor Leisure 31.

*The lovely countryside around Staindrop is seen to advantage on this walk.*

Start: Staindrop Post Office.

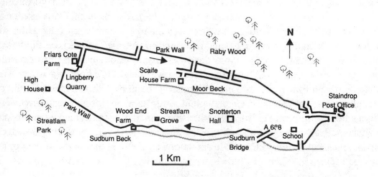

From the Post Office cross the road and the green, and go down the narrow lane next to Scarth Hall. At the bottom turn right to a stile and then bear left across the large field ahead. Go through a gate, cross a stone bridge and bear slightly right to a stile in the hedge opposite. Cross and go towards a double telegraph pole and on to a stile in a stone wall. Cross this, and the minor road beyond, to another stile. Beyond this, continue alongside Sudburn Beck, going through nine small, narrow fields. After about $\frac{1}{2}$ mile, climb some steps to reach the main A688 road at Sudburn Bridge. Cross with care, and go over the old road to a stone stile. Cross and keep straight ahead to cross a wooden stile. Keep close to Sudburn Beck as it bends left. Soon a gate in a stone wall is reached just below the white painted buildings of Snotterton

132

Hall on your right. Go through the gate ahead and cross a footbridge over Sudburn Beck. Continue to a gate, go through and pass the beck on your left and a bank with attractive beech trees on your right. Cross a stile into a field and continue upstream to another gate. Keep in the same direction, crossing two wooden stiles and, once over the second one, bear right, up a bank, to reach the track in front of Streatlam Grove Farm. Go to the left of the farm buildings along a track, edging fields, to Woodend Farm. Keep to the right of the cottage there and cross a stile in the fence to join another farm road. Cross a wooden stile immediately opposite and, keeping in the same direction, aim for a high stone wall in the distance beyond an old bridge. The wall is the boundary wall of Streatlam Park. Follow it through three gates. At a fourth gate the wall changes direction: leave it here and bear right towards a distant plantation of pine trees, just before High House Farm. Before reaching the trees go through a gate in the fence on your right ad along the lovely path past attractive woodland on the site of old Lingberry Quarry. At the end of the wood cross a fence by using stone blocks and continue in the same direction along the left side of the next field. At the bottom turn right and continue along the field edge towards a gate next to a barn. Go through, and continue along a grassy track between a cottage and Friars Cote Farm. Go through another gate and along a farm road to the B6279, the Moor Road. Turn right along it for $^{1}/_{2}$ mile, and go left along a farm track towards West Farm. Where this reaches the high wall of Raby Wood, turn right, over a stile in the hedge. Continue close to the wall on your left, crossing stiles and passing in front of two lodges at private entrances to Raby Wood. At the second lodge go over a wooden stile in front of a vegetable garden and stay close to the wall as you cross two fields. In a third field leave the wall after $^{1}/_{3}$ mile, heading diagonally right to a stile in the field corner. Cross and keep to the edge of the next field to enter another. Soon you go through a gap in the hedge on your right, and along a narrow path, known as 'knicky nack', back into Staindrop (see Notes to Walks 25 and 27) at the corner of North Green. Go down through the village to the post office where the walk began.

REFRESHMENTS:
*The Wheatsheaf Inn,* Staindrop (tel no: 0833 60280).

# Walk 63     BOWES AND GOD'S BRIDGE     7¹/₂m (12km)

Maps: OS Sheets Landranger 92; Outdoor Leisure 30.

*A superb walk which includes some rough moorland.*

Start: The car park, Bowes.

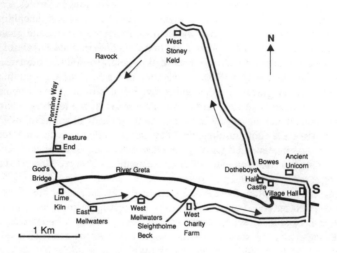

Boots are essential for this walk, which should not be tackled in poor conditions unless you are an experienced walker.

From the car park at the eastern end of Bowes, walk through the village and after passing **Dotheboys Hall** on your left at the western end, follow the road which curves right and crosses the A66 by-pass. Continue along it as it climbs and offers fine retrospective views of Bowes and the moors beyond. Keep with it as it bears left, then right again, passing an old Ministry of Defence site. After about 1¹/₂ miles the road descends and curves left to the entrance to West Stoney Keld. Here keep right to pass through the gate, and then go immediately left to follow a stone wall on the left across open moor. When, after ¹/₄ mile, the wall turns sharp left, bear right, across the moor, and follow a grassy path through heather towards the higher ground of Ravock in the distance. The faint path goes left just beyond a stone grouse butt, and keeps to the

134

drier ground as it passes the remains of two stone walls. Continue in the same direction for $^1/_2$ mile, then turn left, through rough grass, to the corner of a long drystone wall.

Turn right, close to the wall, for $^1/_4$ mile across rising ground to join the Pennine Way at a right-angled bend in the wall. Turn left and go along the side of the wall on our left to join the A66 at Pasture End Farm. Cross the road to a ladder stile and go downhill, keeping to the left of a cottage and going under the old Barnard Castle to Kirkby Stephen railway line. Cross God's Bridge, a natural limestone rock across the River Greta, and go left immediately, through a gate. Bear right past an old lime kiln and continue diagonally right across the field ahead, crossing a rise and going on to the buildings of West Mellwaters Farm. Go to the left of them and keep ahead, across two fields, to reach the farm track to East Mellwaters Farm. There, go between farm buildings and across the yard to enter a field through a gate. Bear slightly left, aiming for a gap in the facing wall, and keep to the right side of the next field with the River Greta just below and on the left. Cross Sleighthouse Beck on a footbridge (Cardwell Bridge) then bear left around the buildings of West charity Farm. Follow Pennine Way arrows past the farm, turning right, then left, to follow a good track for about $1^1/_2$ miles, passing four more farms to reach a minor road at Gilmonby. Turn left, along it, crossing the River Greta, and continue uphill for a short distance to return to the car park.

## POINTS OF INTEREST:
**Dotheboys Hall** – In reality Bowes Academy, this was the notorious school in Charles Dickens famous novel *Nicholas Nickleby*. It was closed soon after Dickens visited it in 1838. It was run by William Shaw and catered for about 100 boys.

## REFRESHMENTS:
*The Ancient Unicorn*, Bowes (tel no: 0833 28321).

# Walk 64  WESTGATE AND ST JOHN'S CHAPEL    7$\frac{1}{2}$m (12km)

Maps: OS Sheets Landranger 92; Outdoor Leisure 31.

*A delightful mix of woodland, moorland and riverside walking, with fine views of Upper Weardale.*

Start: At 905382, the Westgate village car park.

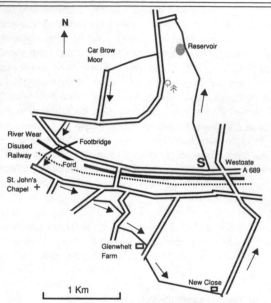

From the car park, opposite a caravan site at the west end of Westgate village centre, take the second turning left, along a minor road to a cluster of houses. Go left, as signposted, to enter a lane through a gate marked 'High Mill Private Land and Gardens'. Continue along a delightful, wooded path, close to a stream on your left, crossing and re-crossing the stream on footbridges to reach some ruins through a white gate. Continue upstream through these ruins, on a clear track to reach a facing stile. Cross to reach open countryside at the valley's head, where grassy spoil heaps and mine entrances litter the valley bottom. Cross a tottery gate in a fence and go upstream as far as a prominent mine entrance, fronted by a grid. There, cross the stream and climb a walled green lane. Turn left at its top end, along another green lane. Walk as far as a gate on your right, the first gate past a solitary hawthorn. Go through this gate and climb to the top left-hand corner of the field ahead. There being no gate, but it being a right of way, cross the wall. Go diagonally left on rising ground. Soon a gate in a facing wall is reached: go slightly right to a gate and through it into a walled lane. Turn left, downhill, to reach a surfaced road. Go right to a footpath sign on the left, from where there is a good view of St John's Chapel below. Turn left down some wall steps into a field, and follow a track diagonally right, over stiles, to a road. Cross as signposted. Cross the field ahead to reach a flight of steps edging a wood on the left. Descend the steps and follow a path to the River Wear, crossing it on a footbridge. Continue in to the village. Go left, bridging a feeder, and left again to pass a small industrial estate on your right. Pass a ford on the left and continue to a stile on the right. Cross and go over the field ahead. Cross a disused railway, then another field to reach a road. Cross the road and go left, briefly, as signposted, then right , again as directed, to a nearby farm. Turn left in front of the farm in to a field. Climb the field, staying close to a wall, then a hedge, on your right, to reach a lane. Cross the lane, pass in front of the farm ahead and cross a garth in to a field. Go over towards a wooded gill, aiming for a lane post proud of the trees. Just beyond the post, bridge the gill and climb the bank ahead to reach a now clearly seen farm. Turn left, briefly, along the farm road to reach a T-junction. Turn right, climbing a steep walled lane. Where the lane turns right at the hill top, go straight ahead to Glenwhelt Farm, bridging another gill en route. Turn right in to the farm yard, cross it diagonally left to a farm road and go right, briefly, then left, as signposted. Now go diagonally right along a faint track around the back of the isolated wood seen ahead. Keeping close to the wood go eastwards, aiming for three ruinous buildings, on the opposite side of a gill ahead. Descend in to the gill, go through a gate in a facing wall and climb steeply to just past the third ruin. Go left, downhill, along a walled lane for about a mile. Once a feeder is crossed, turn right to a road. Cross and bear left to reach Westgate, re-crossing the Wear and going through the village to the car park.

POINTS OF INTEREST:
The mine workings and the course of the railway built to serve them are of great interest to industrial archaeologists.

Throughout the walk the bird life is plentiful and varied.

REFRESHMENTS:
*The Hare and Hounds,* Westgate (tel no: 0388 517212).
*The Golden Lion,* St John's Chapel (tel no: 0388 537231).

# Walk 65     **BOWES AND PASTURE END**     7$\frac{1}{2}$m (12km)

Maps: OS Sheets Landranger 92; Outdoor Leisure 30.

*A nice mix of fell and quiet road walking with an opportunity to test your skill with map and compass on Ravock.*

Start: Bowes Car Park.

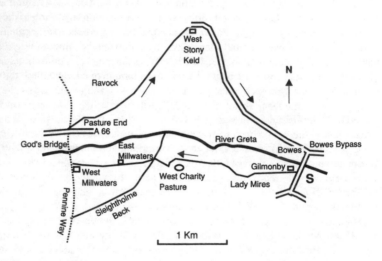

From the Car Park go left along a road signposted 'Gilmonby $\frac{1}{4}$ mile', cross the River Greta on Gilmonby Bridge and enter the hamlet of Gilmonby. At the road signed 'Lady Mires 1 mile: Home Farm – West Gates' turn right along the road for 1 mile, passing West Gates on your right and Lady Mires and West Charity Pasture on your left. Just beyond Lady Mires go through a facing gate on to an unsurfaced cart road and stay with it across two open pastures. As you approach West Charity Pasture Farm watch for a Pennine Way signpost on your right directing you through a gate into the farm, where another Pennine Way sign directs you left by the farm wall to **Cardwell Bridge**. The bridge was built in 1984 to replace the old stepping stones beneath it. Cross the bridge and go through the remains of a wall to a path near a second wall a few yards away. Follow this path uphill with the wall on your left and the River Greta below and on your right. Go through a gate near the telegraph pole and half left over a field to a gate between farm buildings. Go through the gate into the farmyard of East Mellwaters Farm. Turn half right, then left and left again into a gated lane. Continue through two gates and then turn left. Go to the top of the field and through the right-hand of three gates. Turn right along a cart road between gateposts, and go through a gate in the wall on your right. The path passes to the left of West Mellwaters Farm, then goes half right across a field and through a gate to join the main Pennine Way route at God's Bridge. Cross God's Bridge – a natural arch – go over the disused Darlington to Kirkby Stephen railway line and climb to the A66. Cross, with care, to the stile just left of Pasture End Farm. Go over and, keeping close to the wall on your right, go on to the moor, still following the Pennine Way. At the wall corner turn right, away from the Pennine Way and, using a compass, go north-easterly for $1^1/_2$ miles to West Stony Keld Farm. From there take the road, right, for the final $1^1/_2$ miles back to Bowes.

## POINTS OF INTEREST:
**Cardwell Bridge** – The bridge is named after Stan Cardwell, MBE a Darlington man, in recognition of his services to the Rambling Association and countryside conservation.

## REFRESHMENTS:
*The Ancient Unicorn,* Bowes (tel no: 0833 28321).

## Walk 66  BOWES AND SLEIGHTHOLME CIRCULAR  7$\frac{1}{2}$m (12km)
Maps: OS Sheets Landranger 92; Outdoor Leisure 30.
*Good walking along field and farm tracks, over moorland and along a quiet country road.*
Start: The car park, Bowes.

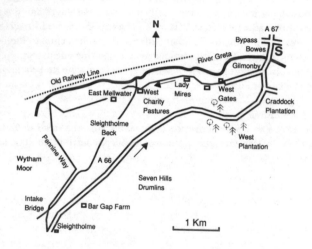

Take the road left from Bowes car park – which is situated at the eastern end of the village – for $\frac{1}{4}$ mile along the Greta to Gilmonby road. Turn right at a sign for 'Lady Mines: 1 mile' and go along a surfaced 'No Through Road' past Gilmonby Farm on your right. Continue westwards, passing West Gates on your right, and West Pastures and Lady Mines on your left. There are good retrospective views to **Bowes**, with its castle, along this section. Keep going westward along an unsurfaced track, keeping watch for a 'Pennine Way' signpost in a wall corner on your right. The sign will direct you to West Charity Pasture Farm. From there follow a sign to Cardwell bridge (see Note to Walk 65), which spans Sleightholme Beck. Cross the footbridge and continue between a wall and some trees, going up a bank. Keep close to a wall, with the River Greta below and on your right. Go through a gateway, then half left over a field to East Mellwaters Farm. Turn right in the farmyard, then left by a brick building and left again, past some sheep pens. Go right into a walled lane going uphill. Continue along this farm road to reach a waymarked stile in the wall to the left of a cattle grid. Cross and continue to West Mellwaters, an old farm, built in 1773 and now being renovated. Beyond the farm go half right across a rough pasture. At its bottom corner, near an old lime kiln you will reach the River Greta where it is spanned by a natural limestone arch known as God's Bridge. The next part of the walk is along the Pennine Way: go southwards up a rough pasture, keeping close to a wall on your left, to reach a ladder stile in a facing wall. Cross and go left for about 200 yards, then right across heather-clad Wytham Moor to Trough Heads, an isolated farmstead overlooking Sleightholme Beck. Turn right near the farmhouse and continue close to the wall on your left to a wooden gate with a 'Pennine Way' sign on its far side. Go through, and continue in the same direction with the wall now on your right and Sleightholme Beck below and on your left. Where the trod descends to cross the beck on Intake Bridge keep straight ahead, crossing a fence, and go through a gate marked 'P-Way'. Cross the field ahead to a gate leading to a moorland road. This is where you part company with the Pennine Way: turn left along the road, passing first Bar Gap Farm on your right, then, also on our right, a group of heather covered drumlins known as the Sween Hills. Follow the road for three miles back to Bowes.

## POINTS OF INTEREST:

**Bowes** – Bowes Castle was built between 1171 and 1187. Close by, the 17th century building on the west end of Bowes, which became the notorious Bowes Academy and was immortalised by Charles Dickens as Dotheboys Hall in *Nicholas Nickleby*, is now privately owned. Between Castle and 'Hall', in St Giles churchyard can be seen the grave of William Shaw, owner/head of the Academy whom Dickens visited while researching his book.

## REFRESHMENTS:
*The Ancient Unicorn,* Bowes (tel no: 0833 28321).

# Walk 67 DURHAM CITY'S MEDIEVAL PILGRIM WALK 7$\frac{1}{2}$m (12km)

Maps: OS Sheets Landranger 88; Pathfinder NZ 24/34.

*A fascinating circular linking the various hospitals founded in the neighbourhood of Durham City during the time of the early Prince Bishops.*

Start: Durham Cathedral.

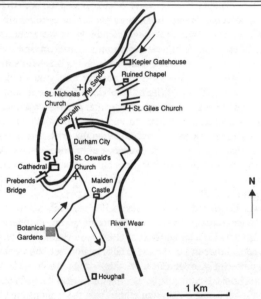

Leave the north door of the **Cathedral** going right, down cobbled Dun Cow Lane to the Church of St Mary-le-Bow. Turn left along North Bailey, passing Hatfield College, and descend through Sadler Street into the Market Place. Continue past St Nicholas Church, cross the main road and go along Claypath. Turn left down Providence Row, a road that curves along The Sands, past the Ferens Park ground of Durham AFC. Just beyond the ground go half-left along a surfaced riverside footpath to where Kepier Hospital gatehouse is seen through the trees. From there go over two stiles, past a farm and left, into open country, still on a surfaced road. When the road ends near the river, turn left over a stile and follow the riverside path back to Kepier. Turn right past the gatehouse, and return to The Sands for 300 yards. Just beyond Orchard Drive take the wide track uphill and continue up steps into a modern cul-de-sac. Go along the cul-de-sac, and turn left, uphill, to a footbridge over the A690, passing, beside the bridge, the ruinous Chapel of St Mary Magdelene Hospital. Cross the bridge and take the path uphill. Turn right near a wooden hall, go along a short pathway into Gilesgate, cross the main road and turn right to the War Memorial. Go briefly uphill to St Giles church. Go past the church tower along a pavement to a gap in a wall. Descend some steps and turn right at the bottom. Continue along a narrow line to the entrance of St Hild and St Bede College. Turn left and descend a stepped path to the riverside. Turn right, cross the Wear on Baths Bridge and turn left along riverside path, passing the old race course on your right. The path eventually curves around, passing a rowing clubhouse. At a cricket pavilion, turn left along a surfaced lane for a few yards, then go right, along a track to the river. Turn right, along the riverbank, passing Maiden Castle, an Iron Age fort. On approaching a bridge follow the track to the right, along the edge of a wood, to the main road. Cross and continue along the path opposite, skirting Great High Wood, for $^3/_4$ mile. Soon after reaching a tall wooden fence on the left, and opposite a bench, cross a stile on the left and go down the right side of a field towards Houghall Farm. Near a post box turn right, cross a stile and go along a path, which rises on to an old wagonway embankment, through fields. At the foot of a hill turn right on to a path through a wood. Stay on it until it begins to climb steeply to join another path. Here turn left, uphill, to reach Hollingside Lane. Turn right and, a little further on, right again, along a gated track next to pyramid-shaped Fountain Hall. Go across the fields, keeping to the right of Mount Joy Research Centre. At a road junction turn right along a footpath, downhill, to Mount Joy Farm. Turn left and go to the main road. Cross and go along a path edged with a stone wall, School Lane, towards the Cathedral to reach Church Street next to St Oswald's school. Cross the road ahead at a refuge and turn right, past St Oswald's Church. At the War Memorial turn into the churchyard and take the path past the church tower to reach the Wear. Cross Prebends Bridge and turn left along a path that climbs past the front of the Cathedral's Galilee Chapel. Beyond the chapel turn right and climb to the Palace Green, next to the University Music School, to end an unusual and informative walk.

## POINTS OF INTEREST:

**Durham Cathedral** – The cathedral which contains the shrine of St Cuthbert, 7th century Bishop of Lindisfarne, is a masterpiece of Norman architecture.

Around Durham various hospitals were founded in the days of the early Prince Bishops. These were originally designed to care for the sick, especially lepers, but as this disease was gradually eradicated the hospitals concentrated more on giving relief to the poor and infirm and offered accommodation to pilgrims.

Walks 68 & 69  **THE LANCHESTER VALLEY RAILWAY WALK**  8m (13km) or 10m (16km)

Maps: OS Sheets Landranger 88; Pathfinder NZ 05/15 & 25/35.

*Along the River Browney valley, following a disused railway.*

Start: At 250415, Broompark Picnic Area.

Finish: Hurbuck Farm or Hownsgill.

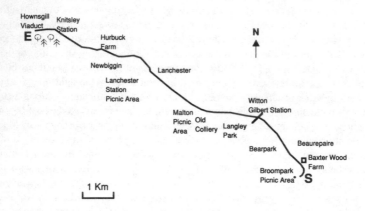

From the Picnic Area go north along the trackbed to the left of; and near, the main East Coast line along which, because it curves at this point, trains are restricted to 70 mph. Soon Quarry House Farm and Baxter Wood Farm are passed, and at both places there are semi-circular 'gin-gan' buildings where horses powered machinery. Beyond Baxter Wood Farm the route curves north-west, and soon passes **Bearpark** village on the left.

The valley of the River Browney, along which the old trackbed threads, is fertile, arable land along its bottom while on the higher, steeper ground the slopes tend to be grazed by cattle and sheep. Some three miles beyond where the route passes Baxter Wood Farm, Witton Gilbert Station is reached and a little beyond it is the car park at

Langley Park. Often, when film makers wanted to portray pit village life, they came to Langley Park. Handball was a popular game amongst Durham's mining community and Langley Park boasts a purpose built handball wall. About $1\frac{1}{2}$ miles beyond Langley Park, Malton is reached. There used to be colliery here, and a benzine works. German engineers built the benzine works and, during World War II, German bombers destroyed it. Malton is now a picnic area, and within another mile the Lanchester Station Picnic Area is reached. Once there was a Roman Fort at Lanchester. Later, and for centuries, it was a busy market town. Today many of the people who live in the village work in Durham City, so mixing town and country life. Because of open cast coal mining further on, the trackbed extends only $1\frac{1}{2}$ miles beyond Lanchester to Hurbuck Farm.

To continue the walk take the temporary footpath – marked by the farmer – that goes northwards from the trackbed to link with a bridleway running parallel to it: the footpath is closed during lambing time. From Lanchester the bridleway can be reached from Kitswell Road, and this provides an alternative route past Hurbuck Farm to Hurbuck Cottages. Turn left at the cottages along a quiet road to Dunleyford. Go right for a mile to a crossroads, and right again to Knitsley Mill. There go left for $1\frac{1}{2}$ miles to reach the point where the Waskerley Way, the Derwent Walk, the Lanchester Valley Walk and the Consett to Sunderland Cycleway will eventually converge.

## POINTS OF INTEREST:

**Bearpark** – The name is a corruption of *Beau Repaire*, which was so named because it was to here that monks came to rest in the country. The remains of Beau Repaire, to the right of the trackbed and on the east side of the River Browney, are open to the public throughout the year: they can be reached by detouring along a footpath from the trackbed.

The old railway, along the trackbed of which the walk passes, was built as cheaply as possible to carry iron ore to Consett. Later the track was doubled to cater for coal traffic from Langley Park.

## REFRESHMENTS:

Pubs and cafés in Lanchester.

Walk 70  **WOLSINGHAM AND TUNSTALL RESERVOIR**  8m (13km)
Maps: OS Sheets Landranger 87, 88 & 92; Pathfinder NZ 04/14
& Outdoor Leisure 31.
*A fairly strenuous field and fell walk, but offering fine views of
Weardale.*
Start: Wolsingham Market Place.

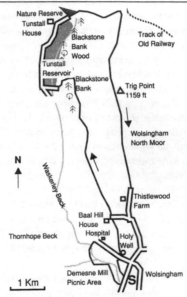

From the Market Place take the B6296, Lanchester road, northwards to the Demesne
Mill picnic area. Turn left through the area and continue upstream close to Waskerley
Beck on your right. In the far corner of the first field go through a kissing gate. Cross
the next field, pass a mill race, cross a stile and go half-left to cross Thurnhope Beck
on a footbridge. Turn right, go through another kissing gate and continue right, along
a field edge path to re-cross Waskerley Beck on stepping stones. Go up the track
ahead to exit opposite Holywood Hall Hospital. Turn right over a stile beside a gate
and go down a lane as far as a footpath sign on your left. Continue up the edge of the
field on your left, climbing steadily, and go through a kissing gate. Bear half left,
towards an isolated gatepost. There, turn right through a wood, and go along a track to

146

Baal Hill Farm (see Note to Walk 45), on your left. Once past the farm take the left of two facing gates, cross a field on a clear, partially walled track, and turn left along a now tree-lined track. Soon after the track turns left, go right, through a gate, to cross Spring Beck. Stay close to a fence to soon reach a clear track that goes through a facing gate and climbs steeply beside Fawn Wood. At a whitewashed farmhouse, turn left along a farm road and cross the dam of Tunstall Reservoir (see Note to Walk 14) on a bridleway. Turn right at the lodge gates to go along the road edging the reservoir for $^1/_3$ mile to a picnic area.

Go through the picnic area and continue northwards beside the reservoir to Tunstall House Farm. Where the road ends, turn right along a rough track. Pass a Nature Reserve – to which there is no access – cross a stone bridge over the top of the reservoir and go through a waymarked gate with the legend 'No road for cars – private'. Climb a steep, unsurfaced track, eastwards, almost as far as the ruins of an old railway depot. Go right, along a track with a wall on your right for guidance, and, after a mile, go through a gate on to Wolsingham North Moor. The path passes close to a trig pillar which, at 1,159 feet is the highest point of the walk. As it leaves the moor through a gate the path broadens into a track which continues downhill for a further $^3/_4$ mile. Leave the track through a gate on to a surfaced lane near Thistlewood Farm. Go along the lane for $^1/_4$ mile, then turn right along another lane to reach Baal Hill House. From here the return route is as the outward one as far as Holywell, where you turn right along a lane for 100 yards. Go left through a gate and diagonally over two fields back into Wolsingham. Turn right to reach the Market Place.

REFRESHMENTS:
There are pubs and a café in Wolsingham, but none on the route.

# Walk 71  St John's Chapel and Burnhope Reservoir  8m (13km)

Maps: OS Sheets Landranger 92; Outdoor Leisure 31.

*A breezy walk through woods, over rough pastures, along quiet roads and the banks of the river Wear.*

Start: The Market Square, St John's Chapel.

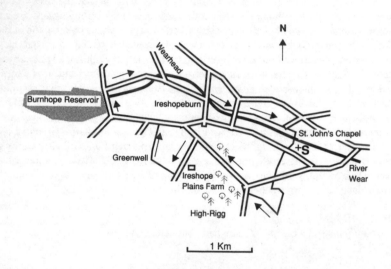

From the chapel in St John's Chapel Market Square, go right, westwards, along the A689. Cross a burn that divides the village and immediately turn left along a signposted footpath with the burn on your left. Continue along this path to some steps. Climb to a kissing gate and go through. Cross the meadow ahead along a path, exiting at a stile in a facing wall. Cross the next field and go through a gate to a road. Cross, going slightly right to a signposted stile near a gate. Cross and continue along a clear path to where a concrete bridge sporting a gate at its middle spans a burn. Cross and follow a climbing path to enter a wood over a ladder stile beside a gate. Go through this delightful wood along a path soft with pine needles and with a murmuring burn below on your right. Climb concrete steps at the end of the wood and descend another flight to recross

148

the burn on a footbridge. Climb a wooded bank using steps, cross a stile in a facing wall and traverse the meadow ahead, close to a wall on your left, to reach a stile near a white gate. Beyond there is a tarmac road: cross close to where another road meets it at a T-junction, and go along this facing road. The road climbs, then descends and passes between plantations. About $1/_2$ mile beyond these, turn left along a farm road to Ireshope Plains. Soon after passing a mast on your right cross a stile, also on your right, and take a rough track across a field to a farmhouse. Go to the left, through a narrow kissing gate, turn right by the side of the house and enter a small field. Cross diagonally left and leave the field at another stile. Descend a depression on the steep, narrow gill ahead, cross Ireshope Burn on a footbridge and turn right, downstream. Cross a small feeder and continue along the burn's bank towards some derelict buildings. Go left there, along a short lane. Turn left at the lane end, going along a quiet lane for 1 mile, and there turn left along another quiet road which crosses the dam of Burn Hope Reservoir. At its northern end, reached after the road turns right, go right along a minor road to reach Wearhead village, about 1 mile distant. There – to the right of a new road bridge over the River Wear, which you do not cross – descend signposted steps to a riverside path. Where this ends at a stile, continue over the field ahead, aiming for a gate where a fence from the river joins a wall. Continue across three more fields on a clear track, crossing stiles and passing to the left of a farm to follow a farm road to a minor road. Turn left and bridge the Wear. Immediately turn right, and continue downstream along a pleasant path, passing Coronation Bridge. A detour over the bridge can be made to the Weardale Museum (see Note to Walk 60). Where a path from the left meets your path at right angles down some steps, turn right along a path that crosses the Wear on a footbridge. Beyond, return to St John's Chapel to end an interesting walk.

**REFRESHMENTS:**
*The Golden Lion,* St John's Chapel (tel no: 0382 537231).
*The Kings Arms,* St John's Chapel (tel no: 0382 537268).
*The Kings Head,* St John's Chapel (tel no: 0382 537237).

# Walk 72    BOWLEES AND THE GREEN TROD    8m (13km)

Maps: OS Sheets Landranger 92; Outdoor Leisure 31.
*Superb walking through heather-clad moorland and over fields.*
Start: The Bowlees Picnic Area car park.

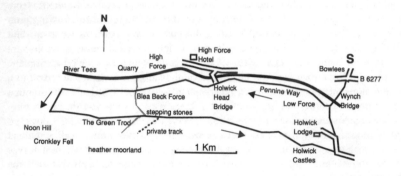

From the car park cross Bowlee Beck and go past the visitor centre to reach a minor road. Go along it to reach the B6277. Cross and go through a kissing gate opposite. Cross two fields on a clear path and continue through trees to cross the River Tees using the Wynch Bridge (see Note to Walk 10) to join the Pennine Way. Turn right, upstream, along the Way, soon passing the beautiful Low Force. Continue along the riverbank to reach Holwick Head Bridge after about 1 mile. Do not cross the bridge: instead go ahead, climbing a slope using a section of path that has been 'stone pitched' to prevent erosion. Continue along a clear path past bird cherry and beech trees and though juniper bushes in Upper Teesdale's National Nature Reserve. Soon the road of High Force (see Note to Walk 24) is heard, and it is glimpsed through the trees. In a short while the path reaches open moor by the top of the falls. The drop at the falls is sheer and long, so please take care if you approach the edge.

Follow the Pennine Way through a pleasant area of rock, bracken and heather, passing a large quarry on the other side of the river to your right. The way soon becomes a grassy track and, after crossing a footbridge, lovely Bleabeck Force is seen to the left. Continue crossing moor footbridge and, still on a clear track, climb the slope ahead, going between more juniper bushes. On reaching the top of this high ground, the white buildings of Forest-in-Teesdale can be seen on the right beyond where the River Tees flows through a gorge. Continue past a small corrugated building and turn left at a waymarker post, leaving the Pennine Way and aiming for a gate in a facing wall. Go through and cross a small stream. Go ahead to a distant Nature Reserve sign beyond where Noon Hill rises. Soon a broad track is seen ahead, crossing your line of walk. Turn left along this – **The Green Trod** – at the Nature Reserve sign and follow it over two streams to climb up the slope alongside a stone wall. At the top, near a cairn, a wonderful view of Teesdale opens out while, to your right, heather-clad moorland stretches into the distance. Continue along this rather wet path to a gate, beyond which cross Blea Beck on stepping stones and go slightly left to join a clear track near a 'No Entry' sign. Follow this track for $1^1/_2$ miles and on approaching the rocky outcrop of Holwick Castle, where it curves left towards Holwick Lodge, go straight ahead, through a gate. Go between the crags to join a tarmac road at the end of Holwick village. After a few yards take the road on your left, and where it curves left continue ahead, over fields and across a stone bridge over a feeder, to return to the Wynch Bridge. Cross and retrace your steps to Bowlees car park.

POINTS OF INTEREST:
**The Green Trod** – The track takes its name from the colour of its grassy surface and is an ancient drove road from Holwick to the Eden Valley. It passes Cauldron Snout and High Cup Nick on its way over the High Pennines.

REFRESHMENTS:
None actually on route, but *The Strathmore Arms,* Holwick (tel no: 0833 40362) lies at the east end of Holwick.

## Walk 73   HAMSTERLEY FOREST AND HIGH ACTON   8m (13km)

Maps: OS Sheets Landranger 92; Outdoor Leisure 31.

*Mainly along forest roads and paths which are waymarked throughout with orange arrows.*

Start: At 053275, Blackling Hole Car Park, Hamsterley Forest.

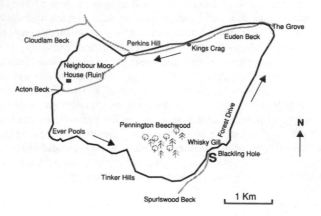

From the car park, near a deep pool beneath a waterfall, take the waymarked path north-east along Spurlswood Beck for $1^1/_2$ miles of pleasant walking to a picnic area called The Grove. From The Grove follow orange arrows up the Euden Beck Valley, passing, after 1 mile, a rocky outcrop on the far side of Euden Beck. The outcrop is known as Kings Crag and is home to several species of fern including the delicate Oak Fern. It is classed as a conservation area. Continue up the beck side for a further $^3/_4$ mile to reach a bridge. Just before the bridge the route passes a section of heathland on the right which, together with the west cliff opposite, form another conservation area where, in summertime, orchids, dragonflies and butterflies can be seen. You are asked not to deviate from the road hereabouts in the interests of preserving wildlife. Cross Euden Bridge and bear right, following Euden Beck, on your right, along a

152

waymarked road, passing Scots Pines on your left. Here keep a look out for short twigs that have snapped off by the wind. If they are hollow, or have a small hole bored in the side, the pine shoot beetle has been busy. These breed under the bark of fallen or felled pines and the adults feed in the shoots of living pines, causing loss of foliage and a check on the tree's growth.

Pass a gate at the end of a forest road and, briefly, join a council road leading to The Grove. Turn right past another gate, and follow a track downhill. Most of the trees on the left of the track are Grand Fir, which are not often grown because the timber is brittle. There are no fallen cones around these trees because they break up while still attached to the tree. Continue along the waymarked paths, passing through stands of mixed broadleaf and coniferous trees. Cross Acton Beck and turn right, leaving the road and following a waymarked path to the forest boundary at Ever Pools, a view point. Continue to **Pennington Beechwood**, from where the forest road is followed back to Blackling Hole.

POINTS OF INTEREST:

**Pennington Beechwood** – One of the highest beechwoods in Britain, at 1100 feet. Other trees to be seen en route include Norway, Sitka, and Serbian Spruces, Scots and Lodgepole Pine and a variety of broad leaves. Winter birds include Crossbills, Siskins and Hen Harriers. In summer there are Wood, Willow and Garden Warblers, Chiff Chaffs and Blackcaps. Roe deer are present all year round.

# Walk 74    MIDDLETON-IN-TEESDALE AND HARDBERRY GUTTER

8m (13km)

Maps: OS Sheets Landranger 92; Outdoor Leisure 31.

*A fine section of Teesdale.*

Start: Middleton-in-Teesdale Car Park.

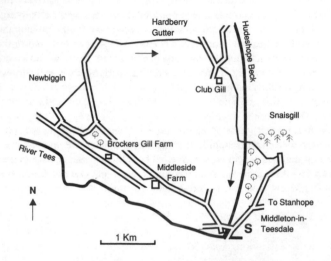

From the car park go along Market Place and fork left across Hudeshope Beck. Continue along a climbing road, and where it divides go right for $^1/_2$ mile. Go past Middle Side Farm, and very shortly reach a milk stand on your left. Go over a facing stile in a step in the wall. Cross the field ahead diagonally left to a gate in a facing wall. Cross the next field close to a wood on your left, leaving over a stile on to a lane. Cross the lane and follow the edge of the next field. Go through a gateway ahead. Walk to within a few yards of a facing wall, and there go left over a stile. Descend the field ahead diagonally to a stile near the lower of two gates seen ahead. Edge the bottom of the next field to reach a wood. There, leave the clear path and go left along a wood edge trod. At a facing wall turn right and descend to a stile near the corner of a facing wall. Cross, and immediately cross the beck to enter Brockers Gill Farm.

154

Cross the farm yard and enter a field through a gate on the right. Go left up a rise and cross the field to a ladder stile. Continue over further ladder stiles to Newbiggin. Turn right between buildings to reach a surfaced road. Go left along the road, passing a road junction and a chapel. Bridge a beck, and immediately go right along the beckside path to reach another bridge. Cross and climb the road to some houses. Go right, through a gate into a field. Turn left, climb to a gate in a wall on your left and go diagonally right to a gateway in the left wall. Continue around an enclosure to double back through another gateway in a continuation of the wall you have just come through. Climb the field ahead and go through a gap in the facing wall. Go diagonally right, on rising ground, to a stile near the top left corner, beyond which go left along a farm track. Go through gates to reach some spoil heaps. At the gate beyond, where the path splits, go straight ahead close to the wall on your right. The great gash on your left as you ascend is Hardberry Gutter. At the brow of the hill, where the wall curves right, walk ahead along a path. Go through a gate in a facing fence. Edge Hardberry Gutter, then alter course to descend roughly parallel to the wall on your right, aiming for a long, straight wall climbing the far side of the valley. Go through a gate in a facing fence and turn right along an unsurfaced track to reach a surfaced road. Continue along it through a gate and go uphill, briefly, to a signposted stile on your left. Cross the field ahead diagonally to a facing stile, and continue in the same direction over rough pasture, crossing a deep gully. Aim for the bottom corner of a facing wall, the easiest place to cross it, the stile having been blocked. Cross the next field going slightly right, to reach a stile. Go directly across the next field to enter woodland over a stile. Immediately go left, between a wall and a fence, passing a prominent ash tree, and, just before a sharp drop, go right down a steep bank, cross a feeder and follow a clear beckside path to a bridge over Hudeshope Beck. Cross and where, almost at once, the track splits, go right, then left, edging woods on your right. Cross some rubble and go right as signposted along a wood edge path that climbs and turn left up the edge of Snaisgill to reach a metalled road. Turn right along it back into Middleton-in-Teesdale.

## POINTS OF INTEREST:
The Methodist Chapel in Newbiggin is the oldest one to have held services continuously since it was built in 1759.

## REFRESHMENTS:
Hotels, pubs and cafés in Middleton-in-Teesdale.

# Walk 75    NANNY MAYOR'S INCLINE    8m (13km)

Maps: OS Sheets Landranger 87 & 88; Pathfinder NZ 04/14.

*A walk with some long climbs, but the reward of extensive views.*

Start: At 077478, the signposted car park on the minor road from Stanhope and Healeyfield to Whitehall and the A68.

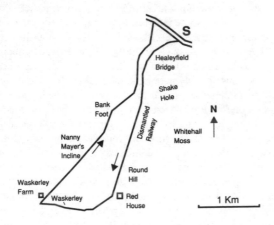

Leave the car park via the picnic area at the west end, and follow the disused railway first west, then south, through a series of cuttings. This is the Waskerley Way, a path following the track-bed of the Stanhope to Consett Railway.

Continue to Red House where you turn right to follow the line of a fence for $^1/_2$ mile to reach the Waskerley Way again. Follow the track west until you reach **Waskerley Farm**.

At the barn turn right, over a stile, and go past the farmhouse and buildings along a grassy track. This is Nanny Mayor's Incline: follow it downhill for $^1/_2$ mile. At the foot, skirt a field, rejoining the track next to a ruin. This was an engine shed, and was in use until 1859.

The track remains obvious though heavily overgrown, and can be followed as

156

far as a stone bridge (Healeyfield Bridge) where you leave it by climbing the steep slope to the left. At the top, cross the stone-wall via a ladder-stile. Keep the wall on your left and follow its line across fields, over the hill to a road. The car park lies $^1/_2$ mile along the road to your right.

## POINTS OF INTEREST:

**Waskerley Farm** – Waskerley was once at the junction of two railways, the Crook to Waskerley and the Stanhope to Consett. The station had sidings, a shed for six engines and wagon repair shops. There was also a village for the families of railway workers, a church, a chapel, a school and shops, all at 1150 feet above sea level.

# Walk 76 STAINDROP, COCKFIELD AND EVENWOOD 8m (13km)

Maps: OS Sheets Landranger 92; Pathfinder NZ 12/13.

*A pleasant, easy walk through the gently rolling south-west Durham countryside.*

Start: Staindrop village.

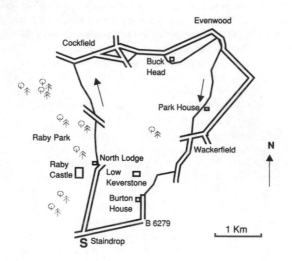

From the east end of Staindrop (see Note to Walk 27) go along the A688, using the roadside footpath, for 1 mile to the North Lodge of Raby Park where, at the Lodge Gates, cross a stile in the wall. Continue northwards on a clear footpath through the wood ahead to reach a minor country road. Cross to a stile. Ignoring the well-defined path going straight ahead, go half-left along a less clearly defined footpath, aiming for a hawthorn tree on the skyline. On reaching this cross a nearby stile and continue towards Cockfield, seen ahead, keeping close to a hedge on your left for two fields. Midway across the third field go half-right towards a row of houses. Cross a stile in the fence ahead, then another in the hedge on your right. Go straight ahead, along a path, across the next field to reach a culvert. There, cross a stile and continue beside the culvert to a street. Turn left into Cockfield, and go right, along its main street, to

158

just beyond the church, on your right. Go through a bridle gate adjoining a field gate, then left to a stile seen in the distance. Cross on to a bridge way. Go over and continue straight ahead, along a clear footpath, to Esperley Lane Ends. Turn right along a minor road. As you pass the last of this row of houses turn left, over a stile, and go forward close to a hedge on your right, to reach the Cockfield to Evenwood Road. Turn right for $\frac{1}{4}$ mile to where the road bends to the left. Cross a stile on your right and go diagonally left, over the field ahead, to Buck Head Farm. Go right, then left, along two sides of a stone wall to reach a stile. Cross and go diagonally left, across the field ahead, to a hedge. Turn left along a clear footpath into Evenwood. At the village green go right, crossing it, and along the street ahead for a few yards to just beyond the corner house of West view. There go along a narrow path leading to fields. Keeping close to the hedge on the right, walk towards the farm ahead and, just before reaching it, cross a stile on your right into a field. Continue close to the hedge on the left along two sides of this field to a corner stile. Cross and turn left along two sides of the field. Cross a stile on your left into another field. Go half-right, and through a large gap in a facing hedge. Go right, close to the hedge on the right, to exit on to a country road. Cross the road and go through either a facing gate or a nearby stile into a field. Go down the field to railings in a corner hedge. Cross and keeping close to the hedge, go along two sides of a field, through a bridleway gate and up the following field to a minor road. Go right, briefly, then left, southwards, towards Wackerfield, passing two road ends on your left. Just beyond the second one, cross a rather indistinct stile on your right. Continue close to the hedge on the left, cross another stile and, now keeping the hedge on your right, walk towards some white farm buildings. There the path turns left for a few yards to reach a stile in the hedge on the right. Cross and go diagonally left, across the next field to a farm road. Turn left to join the B6279. Turn right for $\frac{3}{4}$ mile of grass verge walking back into Staindrop.

## REFRESHMENTS:
There are pubs in Evenwood, Staindrop and Cockfield, and a café in Cockfield.

Walk 77      **MONK'S MOOR**      8m (13km)

Maps: OS Sheets Landranger 92; Outdoor Leisure 31.

*A fine, bracing walk across rough pasture and moorland with some road walking.*

Start: Middleton-in-Teesdale car park.

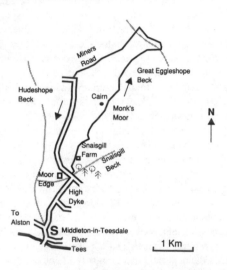

From the car park go northwards, along the main street, past the Cleveland Hotel, and continue up the road signposted to Stanhope, climbing steeply. Go straight ahead, past a road junction on your right, and just beyond where the road bends sharply left, go through a field gate on your right signposted 'Footpath to Frosterly'. Continue on rising ground half left and over a stile in the wall ahead. Go northwards along a faint track close to a shallow depression to a field gate in the wall ahead. Cross the next field to a wall stile, which is crossed to reach open moor. Climbing steadily, continue in a north-easterly direction aiming for a large stone cairn seen on the horizon ahead if the weather is clear. Should poor visibility hide the cairn, walk along a 40° bearing. Just beyond the cairn the summit of Monk's Moor – (1853 feet – 565 metres) is reached. From its broad flat top the views are superb in all directions. Far below, dotted along the lower slopes, are the distinctive white farms of the Raby Estate, many tucked behind protecting belts of trees. Cross the top of the moor, still on a 40° bearing, descending towards the valley of Great Eggleshope Beck. The way is undefined, through heather, on falling ground into the valley where there is much evidence of lead mining days in the form of spoil heaps and ruinous buildings. Cross the narrow beck in the valley bottom on a footbridge. Turn left, upstream, for $^1/_2$ mile to another footbridge and turn left over it. Climb up the shallow gill in front of you along a well defined miner's track, passing a large spoil heap on your left. From the summit of this track the view ahead, down the valley of Hudeshope Beck, open up delightfully. Continue along this miner's track, steeply downhill, to meet a minor road. Turn left along it for $1^1/_2$ miles, back to where you left it on the outward leg, at Snaisgill. The final mile into Middleton-in-Teesdale (see Note to Walk 5) is along the outward route, but this time the going is downhill and much easier.

POINTS OF INTEREST:
The miner's track that climbs from Great Eggleshope Beck over the shoulder of Monk's Moor was constructed by The London Lead Company to carry traffic to and from the nearby lead mines.

REFRESHMENTS:
Hotels, pubs, a café and a fish and chip shop in Middleton-in-Teesdale.

Maps: OS Sheets Landranger 92; Outdoor Leisure 31.
*A tough track following part of the Pennine Way. Be prepared
for rough weather in winter.*
Start: At 810309, the Wheelhead Sike car park.

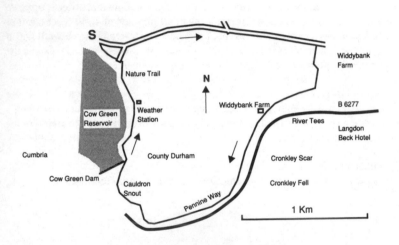

Leave the car park and go along Peghorn Lane for $2^1/_2$ miles. After passing a
whitewashed barn on your left, cross a cattle grid and turn right into an open gateway
displaying one notice which says 'Grazing Stock – all dogs must be on a lead' and
another saying 'Cauldron Snout Fall'. Take this winding farm road into Upper Teesdale
National Nature Reserve, passing another sign which states 'Cauldron Snout $3^1/_2$ miles'.
Continue along the lane, passing yet another sign, this time on a breeze block barn.
This one states 'Cauldron Snout 2 miles'. Along this section there are some fine
views of Upper Teesdale, dotted with the whitewashed farms of the Raby Estates. At
the end of the farm road, which is one mile long, isolated, whitewashed Widdybank
Farm and the Pennine Way are reached. Go through the farmyard, following Pennine
Way signs along a gravel track, and cross the stile in the corner of the wall, the only

stile throughout the walk. Take the path beside the River Tees, going upstream through pleasant green pastures and with the heights of Widdybank Fell on your right. The path skirts the tall Falcon Clints, the foot of which is boulder strewn. Some parts of the route at this point is along duck-boards. As you round a bend in the river and the confluence of the River Tees and Maize Beck is reached, **Cauldron Snout** looms ahead. Scramble up the eastern side of the fall, crossing well worn rocky outcrops. Take care while doing this because the rocks can be slippery and muddy in wet weather. Ahead is the dam at the head of Cow Green Reservoir: turn right below it, along the surfaced nature trail. Stay with this, close to the reservoir on your left, for $1^1/_2$ miles, leaving it through a kissing gate. Turn right up a gravel path, which was once a miner's tramway used to carry barytes from nearby disused lead mines, to return to the car park.

POINTS OF INTEREST:
**Cauldron Snout** – The fall, which cascades down 200 feet of Great Whin Sill, is one of the most impressive waterfalls in Britain. From the top of the fall there is a good view of Mickle Fell, at 2591 feet the highest summit in Durham.

Until several years ago when all the county boundaries were altered the confluence of the River Tees and Maize Beck was where the counties of Durham, Westmorland and Yorkshire met. Today only Cumbria and Durham meet there.

The nature trail offers excellent views of some of the highest summits on the Pennines: Knock Fell, Great Dun Fell and the highest of them all, Cross Fell.

REFRESHMENTS:
*The Langdon Beck Hotel,* Forest-in-Teesdale (tel no: 0833 22267).
*Widdybank Farm.* Tea, coffee and snacks. All walkers and dogs on leads welcome.

## Walk 79  STANHOPE DENE AND CRAWLEY EDGE  8m (13km)

Maps: OS Sheets Landranger 87 & 92; Pathfinder NY 84/94 & Outdoor Leisure 31.

*A fairly strenuous walk through woodland and across pathless moor.*

Start: Stanhope Market Place.

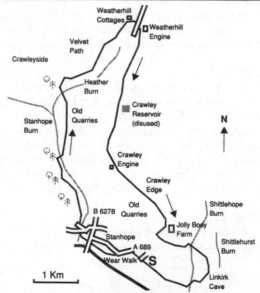

From the Market Place go down The Butts to the River Wear, then upstream along the tree-lined Wear Walk to the Memorial Fountain. Turn left briefly along the A689. Cross Stanhope Burn Bridge and turn right into a signposted lane. Go northwards along it past the Mill and through an open gateway. Go right, then left along Stanhope Burn. Ignoring a footbridge over the burn, take the perimeter path upstream, passing a misleading yellow arrow on a gate post. Keep on the fenced path, turn right through a rusty gate and continue uphill on an enclosed path to re-enter Stanhope Dene by plank bridge. Climb uphill through the wood and where the path bifurcates take the lower route down to Stanhope Burn. Cross on a footbridge, and climb steeply up steps out of the valley on to a quarry road. Turn left along the road for ¹/₂ mile to

164

Stanhope Burn Mine. There, turn right, then left, along a stony track. Go through a metal gate on to open moor. Keep on the track, which curves right, uphill, close to a stone wall. Where the wall goes right and downhill, continue along the track, now a thick, springy trod known as **The Velvet Path**, in an easterly direction and turn left, up a small gill, just short of an old railway wagon. Climb across tussock grass, up the pathless moor, in a north-easterly direction to reach Weatherhill Cottages and **Weatherhill Engine**. Cross the B6278 and head southwards, downhill, along the disused Stanhope and Tyne Valley Railway for $1^1/_2$ miles, going parallel to the B6278. As you approach a partially renovated house, turn left along a track, through gateposts and then right, past the house's garden wall. Stay on the track, which curves left, eastwards, along Crawley Edge. Continue above Ashes Quarry and after 1 mile, when the track bifurcates, go half-right below a walled enclosure. Just beyond a little wood, turn right, downhill, and then left along a track near Craig Cottage. Now cross a stile and exit opposite Jolly Body Farm. Go down a lane leading to Stanhope as far as a cottage, Isengard, on your right. There, cross a stile on your left and take a path eastwards over four stiled fields. Once over a partly painted, white stile go half-right, cross another stile, and go down a wooded, beckside path. Cross Shittlehope Burn on a footbridge and climb out of the gill on a stepped path. Cross another stile, go half-right over a field and exit through a broken gate. Turn left up the next field, past ruinous Ravensfield Farm, and cross a fence near another empty house. Turn right, down a meadow, and right again past a farm entrance. Cross a facing stile to reach a sunken lane. The way forward is down it but the going is much easier along its outside. Cross Shittlehope Burn on a footbridge, go over the field ahead and leave it between two bungalows. Turn left down Woodcroft Gardens to reach the A689 and go right along it back into Stanhope.

POINTS OF INTEREST:
**The Velvet Path** – The path is part of an old packhorse trail.
**Weatherhill Engine** – The stationary engine sited at Crawley Engine, close to the walk, was used to haul wagons up the steep incline from the quarry below. From there to Weatherhill Engine the wagons were hauled by another stationary engine, or by horses or gravity.

REFRESHMENTS:
There are hotels, pubs and cafés in Stanhope.

# Walk 80 SHERBURN AND PITTINGTON CIRCULAR 9m (14.5km)

Maps: OS Sheets Landranger 88; Pathfinder NZ 24/34.

*A pleasant walk along field and woodland paths linking several villages in the former colliery country of east Durham.*

Start: Sherburn.

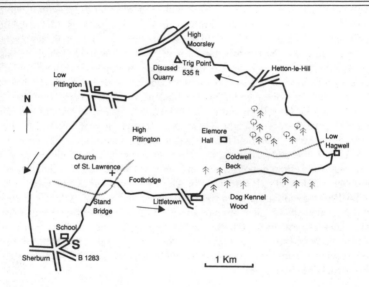

Leave Sherburn along the Pittington road and almost opposite the George Parkinson Memorial Homes go right, along Hall Gardens. Turn left through double metal gates at the end of the school playing fields and take a path northwards to Coldwell Beck. There go right, along the beck side, to Stand Bridge, a metal footbridge. Cross and go along a clear path over the brow of a hill. Cross a large corner stile, and go half-right along a curving path to the hamlet of Hallgarth. Take the enclosed path outside the churchyard, cross a bridge and follow a field edge path past Littletown Farm and some terraced houses to enter a lane through a kissing gate. Continue half left, uphill to the top of a field. Go through another kissing gate and along a sandy track to the Pittington Road. Cross the road to reach the Duke of York, a popular pub. From the pub go along Plantation Avenue and bear left between garages. Cross a waymarked stile, traverse some scrubland, go over a bridge and through a white gate. Turn left into Dog Kennel Wood and follow the rutted track indicated by a yellow waymarker on a tree. Keep along the track, just inside the wood, and go between stone gate pillars into the grounds of **Elemore Hall**. Go past the former farm buildings of Elemore Grange and descend to a junction of three paths. Ignore the path on the right, cross a beck and, ignoring the path on the left, take the next on the right. Climb the path as it winds along the beck, and leave the wood over a stile. Continue along the wood's edge and turn left, along a sandy, gated track, climbing steeply, towards Low Haswell Farm. Just before it, cross a stile near a green gate, and turn half-right across three stiled fields, going downhill. Cross a concrete bridge in the valley bottom to enter East Wood. Turn right for a few yards, then left, through the wood, climbing steeply, to exit over a stile. Go ahead, down a path alongside the wood to a large gap. Turn right along a farm track to Hetton le Hill. Go left through the hamlet to Bramble House. Turn right along the road for 50 yards to a signposted stile on the left. Cross and take the path ahead, which deteriorates to a track alongside a field. Ignore the waymarked stile on your left, and turn right by the fence on your right. Go over a waymarked stile on your left and turn right by the fence on the right. Follow a waymarked path on rising ground, curving westwards, to High Moorsley. Cross the road, and a signposted stile near a post box. Descend a hillside path and at the bottom turn left along a level path back to the Pittington Road. Cross to reach a signposted stile. Cross and follow the path ahead, passing a disused quarry to reach another stile. Cross, turn right over a second stile and descend between bushes. When the path levels out watch for a kissing gate on your right, from which an enclosed path leads to Low Pittington. Turn right along the street to the Blacksmith's Arms, and go left there, along Sherburn Road. After a short distance go through a gate on your right and along a path which, after $1/_2$ mile, merges with a disused railway. Go past the ruins of an old mill and on for $1/_2$ mile. As you approach a railway bridge, go left, uphill, and walk parallel to a railway line. Soon the path you are on veers left to reach Sherburn.

## POINTS OF INTEREST:
**Elemore Hall** – The Hall, now a special school, is where, in 1792, Anne Elizabeth Milbanks, the wife of the poet, Lord Byron, was born.

## REFRESHMENTS:
*The Duke of York,* Littleton (tel no: 091 372 0440).
*The Blacksmith's Arms,* Low Pittington (tel no: 091 372 0287).
*The Grey Horse,* Sherburn (tel no: 091 372 0387).
*The Squire Trelawney Restaurant,* Sherburn

# Walk 81     SUMMERHOUSE AND HILTON     9m (14.5km)

Maps: OS Sheets Landranger 92 & 93; Pathfinder NZ 12/13, NZ 01/11 & NZ 21/31.

*A pleasant walk, mostly along narrow country lanes.*

Start: At 202192, the Raby Hunt Inn, Summerhouse.

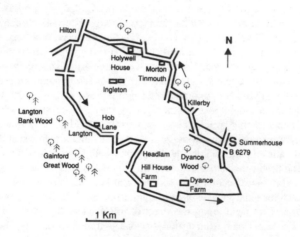

From the Inn go northwards, through the hamlet, to a stile in a wall at its left-hand corner. Cross and continue westwards, close to a hedge, first on your left, then on your right, to join a quiet lane. Go right through Killerby. Turn left at the top of the hamlet for a few yards, then cross a corner stile on your right. Go across the middle of the field ahead to a stile and a footbridge over a ditch. Continue in the same direction to reach a lane over a stile with an attached metal gate. Turn right along the lane for $^1/_2$ mile to reach the little community of Morton Tinmouth. Turn left along the road to Hilton. Where the road turns sharp right, keep straight ahead, through a field gate, and continue close to a hedge on your right to Hollywell House. Go between the farm buildings and, keeping in the same direction, continue past a disused quarry on your right to reach two facing gates. Go through the one on the right, then half-right, uphill, and through a field gate in the top corner of the field into a lane. Turn left, passing Hilton Hall, to reach Hilton. At the far end of the village turn left along another country lane to a junction. Turn right as far as another junction. Go left and follow this quiet lane, crossing the B6279 (Darlington to Staindrop) road and passing, first High Hulam Farm, then Langton hamlet, to reach a T-junction. Turn left along a narrow, green lane known as Hob Gate to reach the Ingleton to Gainford Road. Cross to reach Back Lane, and go along it for almost $^1/_4$ mile. Turn right, over a stile in a hedge just beyond a bridge over Langton Beck. Go diagonally left over the field ahead to reach a stone stile near a house. Cross this stile to reach Headlam. Cross the village green to Headlam Hall and turn right along the road. Where, after bending sharp right, the road bifurcates, go left, passing, on your right, the entrance to Burn House Farm, and, on your left, the entrance to Hill House Farm. About $1^1/_2$ miles from Headlam, turn left along the farm road to Dyance Farm. Go past the farmhouse and the right of the farm buildings, then diagonally right, aiming for a stone wall edging Dyance Wood, where a cart road is reached. Go along it, through a field gate and around two sides of the field ahead, back into Summerhouse.

## POINTS OF INTEREST:
The good views of distant Richmondshire and Teesdale, the unspoiled pastoral flavour of the surrounding countryside and seeing at first hand several small farming communities, combine to make this was a very pleasant outing.

## REFRESHMENTS:
*The Raby Hunt Inn,* Summerhouse (tel no: 0325 74604).

Walk 82          **BURNHOPE BURN**          9m (14.5km)
Maps: OS Sheets Landranger 87; Pathfinder NY 84/94 and
NZ 04/14.
*A walk with moorland, solitude and magnificent views. You will
need map and compass.*
Start: At 015499, St Edmund's Church, Edmundbyers.

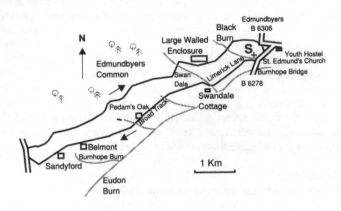

Leave Edmundbyers along the B6278. Where the road bends left, turn right into
unsignposted Limerick Lane. Go along this unsurfaced, gated lane and after a mile
cross a small burn and go up a fairly steep, stony track, past Swandale Cottage, on
your left. At the top of the hill turn left by derelict College Farm. Continue westwards
along a bridleway for 1 mile and, as you approach the next farm, go through the left of
three metal gates and pass in front of derelict **Pedam's Oak Farm**. Go through two
farm gates, cross Pedam's Oak site, and climb the track away from it. Go through
another gate and straight ahead for a further mile to Belmont, another abandoned
farm. Turn right, passing the farm on your left, cross a stile near a gate and go left
along a rutted track. At a padlocked gate, pass it on your left and go right, up a track.

170

Cross a stile beside a facing wall, near a Parish Boundary Stone which looks like a headstone and carries the letters LC and DC. Keep straight ahead to reach the Stanhope-Blanchland road and turn right along it, briefly, as far as a bridleway signpost. Turn right on to Edmundbyers Common. At first the way, ENE, is undefined, but soon a thin path is reached. This path becomes a broad track as you approach a line of butts. Go through a gate in a facing wire fence and along a clear, moorland track for a mile. Go through a gate in a boundary fence and turn left across a rough pasture. Leave the pasture's eastern end over a stile in a wire fence to return to the moor. Follow a moorland path for 1 mile, crossing Swan Dale Burn, beyond which the track goes right, above Limerick Edge, passing a large walled enclosure on the left. Keep to the track, downhill, to cross Black Burn. Follow a gated bridleway to reach the B6306, the Blanchland road. Go downhill into **Edmundbyers** village and the end of a lovely walk.

## POINTS OF INTEREST:
**Pedam's Oak Farm** — A farm has occupied this site continually since 1380. The now derelict house was named after a horse thief, who hid in a now gone oak tree.
**Edmundbyers** – The village Youth Hostel is a converted pub, the Old Low House Inn, built in 1600. The 40 bed hostel, opened in 1936, is haunted by a Londoner who died of exposure while looking for his girl friend on the fells. There is a moral there, somewhere. St Edmund's Parish Church is early 12th century.

## REFRESHMENTS:
*The Punch Bowl,* Edmundbyers (tel no: 0207 55206).

# Walk 83   COTHERSTONE AND THE RIVER BALDER   9m (14.5km)

Maps: OS Sheets Landranger 92; Outdoor Leisure 31.

*A pleasant walk close to the north bank of the Balder.*

Start: Cotherstone Church.

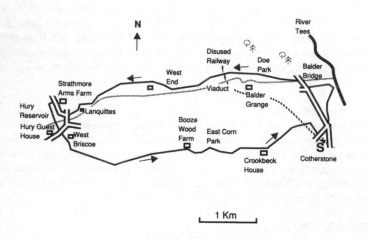

From the church go right to the B6277. Where the road curves left go right between houses at a 'To the Mill' sign. Where this road goes right, turn left along a lane to a yard. Turn right into a field. Continue to a fence corner on your left and go left through a gate into the next field. Cross diagonally right to a stile. Cross and turn right along a track to a stile left of a house. Go uphill on a broad track and where this turns right go left down a stepped path to the confluence of the rivers Tees and Balder. Turn left along a road and just beyond a wooden house go right, crossing a field to a road bridge. Go right across it. Turn left over a stile and, following a yellow marker, cross the valley and climb from it through a gap in its wooded rim. Go along the edge, crossing waymarked stiles. When Balderdale viaduct is seen ahead, aim for a twin telegraph pole and cross the stile just before it. Cross the disused railway and go over the next field to a gate in its left corner. Go left along the track to West End Farm. By the farmhouse turn right across the farmyard into a pasture. Go left to a gate and across the field ahead passing a depression. At a waymarked gate stay close to a fence on the left and head to an outbuilding. Turn right at a waymarker over a broken wall. Go diagonally left towards a gill and cross a waymarked stile half hidden by hawthorns. Cross a beck and go diagonally left to a wall. Go right along it and, keeping to the left of a wall ahead, descend to a wooded gill and bridge over the beck. Climb the far bank, go through a waymarked gate, pass an outbuilding and go along a farm road to a gate beside the Balder on your left. Follow the road uphill. Just before Strathmore Arms Farm turn left and cross the dam of **Hury Reservoir** going left at Hury Guest House. Go briefly along a road and then right, through a gate, along a farm road. Go through West Brisco farmyard, leaving through two gates left of the farmhouse. Cross the pasture ahead to a gate on to moorland. Go left on a bearing of 148° to a distant railway van. There alter course to 78° and cross How Beck on a footbridge. Go east along a water course, then, guided by an outbuilding ahead, leave the water course and on reaching the moor's edge go right along a farm road. Where this goes left into Booze Wood Farm ignore the signposts and stay by the wall on your left which soon curves left. On reaching Cuckoo Cottage go left through a gate and down a field, staying by a wall on the right to reach a road. Turn right, pass a cottage, and cross the facing field diagonally left to a gate near its bottom corner. Cross the next field to a gate. Go through and right to a fence. Go left along this to a stile in a wall. Cross a field. Go diagonally right across the next field and through a gate in a wall. Turn left to another gate, beyond which go diagonally left to the corner gate of a rough pasture. Stay close to a wall on the left to reach a stile at a wire fence. Cross two fields, exiting at a ruinous stile. Cross the next field, passing Crookbeck Farm on your right, to reach a stile. Cross three more stiled fields. In the fourth field past the farm, go diagonally left to a stile. Cross the next field diagonally left to its bottom corner. Turn right by a stream and go through a gate. Cross the next field keeping close to a wall, then a fence on your left. Go through a gap in a railway embankment. Cross the field ahead, curving right. Go through a gate to a road and turn left back to Cotherstone Church.

POINTS OF INTEREST:

**Hury Reservoir** – Stocked with rainbow and brown trout by the Northumberland Water Authority. They issue daily fishing permits: fly and worm only.

REFRESHMENTS:

*The Hury Guest House,* Hury Reservoir
*The Fox & Hounds,* Cotherstone (tel no: 0833 50241).
*The Red Lion Hotel,* Cotherstone (tel no: 0833 50236).

# Walk 84   HURY RESERVOIR AND BIRK HAT   9m (14.5km)

Maps: OS Sheets Landranger 92; Outdoor Leisure 31.

*An exhilarating walk.*

Start: At 968192, the Car Park on the south side of Hury Dam.

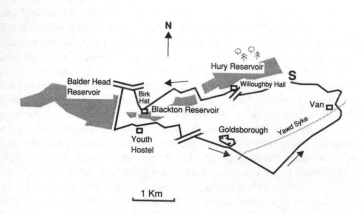

Leave the car park left, briefly, along the road to a footpath sign. Go right to West Brisco and near a farmhouse turn right again, through a gate. Go over a stile and cross a field, edging a wall on the right. Where it ends go ahead, left of a field house, to reach a stile. Cross a field to a stile. Cross and stay close to the wall on your left, passing a field house. Cross another field towards some buildings. At the first one go left through a gate, and continue left of ruins. Cross a stile in a facing wall. Pass a byre and immediately go right, through a gate, and diagonally left across a field to a gate in the corner leading to a minor road. Go left, and just past a farmhouse, right, go up some steps and over a stile.

Cross the field ahead diagonally left to a gate in a facing wall. Beyond go left along a road edging Hury Reservoir. Take the downhill fork, cross the dam and bear left along a bridle path to Blackton Reservoir. Go right through a gate and diagonally

174

left across the next field to exit at a corner gate. Continue along a lane to a gate. Turn left close to a hedge on your right. Go through a gate in the facing wall and along a green track. Go through the right-hand of two gates in a facing wall. Edge the next field and go along a short lane, leaving it over a footbridge. Continue across the field ahead. Go through a gate right of a field house and cross the next two fields. Bear left in the third to reach **Birk House**. Turn right along a farm road to reach a minor road to Baldershead Reservoir. Turn left into the grounds, cross the dam and turn left along an unsurfaced road through the Youth Hostel grounds. Beyond, where the road splits, go right and soon after bridging a beck, go left, following a signpost for Bowes Loop. The path leads to a stile. Cross and go diagonally left across the next field to a stile. Cross another, bridging a beck, to reach a stile in a facing wall. Continue to a stile near the right-hand corner of the next field and continue over stiled fields to a stile backed by trees at East Friar Farm.

Go behind the farmhouse, then right through a gate to farm road that first fronts it, then climbs left to a minor road. Turn left for 200 yards, then right at a signpost. Follow a moorland path that joins a broader one at a tangent. Keep along this to the top of Goldsborough. Descend its southern edge to join a path meandering south-easterly to cross Yawd Sykc after $^1/_3$ mile. Roughly midway between this syke and a facing wall, go left along an undefined route to the outward corner of a wall clearly seen ahead. Continue close to the wall on your right, parallel to the syke on your left, to where a railway wagon is reached on its far bank. Here cross the plank bridge and go right, downstream, to a ruin. From there curve left along a track to a road. Where this curves right, cross a facing stile and go across the field ahead to reach a stile near an electricity pole on the left. Continue up the field ahead, following a line of poles. On reaching West Bisco turn right into the farmyard and rejoin the outward route.

POINTS OF INTEREST:
**Birk Hat** – This was Hannah Hauxwell's farm. The reclusive star of *So Long a Winter* now lives in Cotherstone.

REFRESHMENTS:
Hury Reservoir tea-rooms.

# Walk 85  LANGLEYDALE COMMON AND WOODLAND FELL  9m (14.5km)

Maps: OS Sheets Landranger 92; Outdoor Leisure 31.

*A fairly strenuous walk with lots of rough pasture.*

Start: At 060218, a T-junction ¹/₂ mile east of Kinnivie.

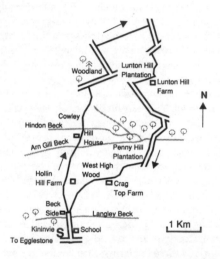

Kinninvie is a hamlet on a crossroads roughly midway between Staindrop and Eggleston, on the B6279. From the road end go north along a narrow lane. Pass a small school building on your right, cross Langley Beck and pass Beckside on your left. Where the lane turns right, continue straight ahead over two fields staying close to a hedge on your left. In the third field go diagonally right towards a small building seen in the distance. Hold this course across two fields to reach Arn Gill Beck. Cross the beck on a small bridge and go ahead near a wall on your right. Go through a bridle gate and pass Hill House Farm on your left. Turn half-right and continue northwards, crossing first a stile, then Hindon Beck on a footbridge, to reach Cowley Farm. Go between the farm buildings and down the next field, staying close to a fence on your right to reach a stile. Cross and maintain the same direction, crossing a succession of stiles, to reach a footpath leading into **Woodland**. Go right, along the village street, then left, along a road signposted to Hamsterley. After $^1/_2$ mile, just short of the second farm on your left, cross some railings on your right and go ahead, close to a wall – first on your left, then on your right – to reach a lane. Turn right and go along the lane to join a minor road. Turn right for 100 yards, then left, through a gate into a field. Continue along a path close to a hedge on our right. Go through the field gate ahead on a path that curves right to join the farm road to Lunton Hill Farm. Stay on this farm road, going round the back of the farm buildings. Go diagonally across the next field to the corner of Lunton Hill Plantation and straight ahead, close to a hedge on your left, to reach a minor road. Turn left, passing Copley village after almost 1 mile, and descend into Arn Gill to bridge the beck and climb steeply out of it. A further $^1/_2$ mile from the gill turn right, through a field gate, and go along a path, keeping close to Penny Hill Plantation on your left, and crossing three fields. Still on the path, leave the wall and go diagonally left to Crag Top Farm. The way is now around the back, and by the far side, of the farm buildings, then westwards, close to a wall on your left, to West High Wood Farm. Again go around the back and down the far side of the buildings, and then along the farm road to the second field. Cross this diagonally left, going through two bridge gates close to a small plantation on your left. Maintain your south-westerly direction, passing Hollin Hill Farm over on your right, to rejoin the tarmac lane at Beck Side. From there retrace your steps to the road end where it all began.

POINTS OF INTEREST:
**Woodland** – Sited 1,150 feet above sea level, Woodland is the highest village in County Durham. Once it was a flourishing mining community, but with the closing of the local coal mines in the 1920's the population declined.

REFRESHMENTS:
*The Edge Hotel*, Woodland (tel no: 0388 718873).

# Walk 86     MEETING OF THE WATERS     9m (14.5km)

Maps: OS Sheets Landranger 92; Outdoor Leisure 31.

*An easy riverside walk.*

Start: Galgate, Barnard Castle.

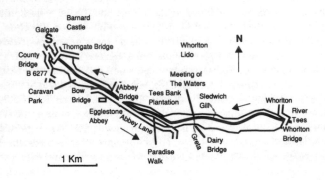

From Galgate, Barnard Castle's main street, go between the Post Office and Trinity Methodist Church to Scar Top park, and downhill beside the castle. Cross the Tees on the County Bridge and turn left along the B6277 almost as far as a Z-road sign to turn left to a gated stile. Go over to a caravan park. Go along a tarmac road and cross a waymarked stile in the fence on your left. Continue eastwards over four stiled fields, following yellow arrows, to reach Abbey Lane over a stile, slightly upstream of Bow Bridge, a 17th century packhorse bridge. Egglestone Abbey, on your right, is well worth a visit (see Note to Walk 9). Rejoining the lane, continue eastwards along it for $^1/_4$ mile to reach Abbey Bridge. Do not cross: instead, go through a gate at the southern end and take the wooded riverside path for 1 mile. When the gravel path ends, continue by the river's edge. Cross Manyfold Beck, climb up a field and continue through woodland to Mortham Lane. Go left along it for $^1/_2$ mile to the **Meeting of the Waters**, where the Greta flows into the Tees. Go right along the Greta to Daisy Bridge, cross it and follow the drive signed 'Mortham Tower'. Where it curves right, turn left to reach a waymarked stile. Cross and go eastwards, along the edge of the next two stiled fields, following yellow arrows. In the third field curve left and go along a track close to a wall on your left, passing ruinous West Thorp Farm. Go through a gap in the corner of the field and along the edge of another field. Exit through a waymarked gate and go diagonally, half left, across a pasture to reach a road, on the far side of which is **Whorlton Lido**. Turn left along the road, cross the Tees over **Whorlton Bridge** and, near a toll cottage, climb to Whorlton village. This is the walk's half way point and refreshments can be found at the Bridge Inn. Leave Whorlton along a signposted path near the 'Whorlton' sign by the top of wooded Whorlton Banks. Follow yellow markers and waymarked stiles, along the edges of four fields, to go down an enclosed path and past a row of oak trees. Beyond these curve left to a blue gate. Continue westwards along a path beside a wood and across stiled fields. At a public footpath sign cross a stile and take the woodland path down to Stedwich Gill. Cross and climb steeply to a stone wall stile. Cross and go over four fields, using stiles or gates. At a double stile veer right close to a stone wall, cross a stile at the end of the field, and go half left across the next field to another stile. Again go half left, to a corner stile above Tees Bank Plantation. Follow a path westwards across three fields. Now bear left, downhill, to a corner gate and go across a field and over a stile to a road. Turn right along it to where it goes right, near a wooden seat, and turn left there, through a waymarked kissing gate. Now follow the clear path upstream back into Barnard Castle (see Note to Walk 36) and the start of the walk.

## POINTS OF INTEREST:
**The Meeting of the Waters** – This spot has inspired many poets and painters, Joseph Turner's watercolour study of Daisy Bridge being particularly fine. Sir Walker Scott wrote about it in his lengthy poem *Rokeby*.
**Whorlton Lido** – The Lido is a leisure recreation park.
**Whorlton Bridge** – A suspension bridge which is 32 feet high, has a span of 180 feet and was once a toll bridge. Work started on it in August 1830 and the bridge was completed in July 1831.

## REFRESHMENTS:
There are a lot of hotels, pubs and cafés in Barnard Castle.
*The Bridge Inn,* Whorlton (tel no: 0833 27341).

# Walk 87  BISHOP AUCKLAND AND PAGE BANK  9m (14.5km)
Maps: OS Sheets Landranger 92 & 93; Pathfinder NZ 12/13 & NZ 23/33.

*An easy to follow walk mostly along disused railway lines.*
Start: Bondgate car park, Bishop Auckland.

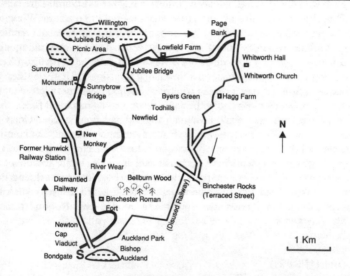

Leave the car park right, along High Bondgate and down Bridge Street. Go half right to join the disused railway line to Brandon. Follow the line northwards, crossing to arched Newton Cap viaduct, which spans the River Wear. Continue along the old line for $1^1/_2$ miles to reach the former Hunwick station, now a private house. Continue for a further $^1/_2$ mile to where, at a bench seat on the left, you leave the line going right, along a field and woodland path to the Wear. If you miss this turn off, continue along the line to where a Public Footpath sign directs you down a track. Where this turns right go ahead, over a stile and along the side of a field on a beck side path to the river. Where the route from the bench seat reaches the river continue upstream past Furness Mill Farm to Sunnybrow Bridge, where the alternative route is joined. From Sunnybrow Bridge, known locally as the Pay Bridge, an interesting diversion can be made bearing left, uphill, to a replica of a coal wagon on a concrete plinth. It was erected in 1976 to commemorate the Rocking Strike of 1863. Back at the bridge the way is along the riverside to the **Jubilee Bridge** picnic area. Beyond this, cross the road ahead, pass the sewage works and continue along a rutted riverside path. Go behind the disused **Skittswood Pumping Station** and through a kissing gate. Where the river curves sharply to the right leave it and walk towards the uphill side of some hawthorns seen ahead. Turn left at a fence corner and keep close to it to Lowfields Farm. Turn right in front of some houses and continue along the edge of a field to reach the Wear at a kissing gate. Take the gated track close to the river on your right for about a mile to reach Page Bank, a pit village. Go right, across the River Wear, and along steep Whitworth Road, passing, after $^1/_2$ mile, **Whitworth Hall**. At Whitworth Church turn right into Hagg Lane and continue along it to where it bends right. There go sharp left up a path to the right of a hedge, to reach another disused railway line. Cross and turn right along the line for $^1/_4$ mile. Cross the road ahead into Byers Green picnic area. Continue along the track bed past the remains of Byers Green station. Cross the Binchester Road; pass Binchester Rocks, a terraced street, on your left, and continue southwards for a mile, going under two bridges. Close to a third bridge go left up steps, then left along the embankment to cross the disused line on the middle of the three bridges. Follow yellow waymarkers cross four fields close to Auckland Park Boundary wall. When the road along the River Wear is reached, close to where the Rivers Gaunless and Wear merge, turn left along the road to enter Bishop Auckland up steep Wear Chase. Continue to the start point.

POINTS OF INTEREST:
**Jubilee Bridge** – The bridge was built for Queen Victoria's Golden Jubilee in 1887.
**Skittswood Pumping Station** – Used until the 1960's to pump water to Brancepeth Colliery.
**Whitworth Hall** – The original Hall was destroyed by fire and totally rebuilt in 1877. It was the ancestral home of the Shaftos, the most famous of whom was Bobby Shafto of ballad fame.
From the road back into Bishop Auckland there is an impressive view of Auckland Castle, the residence of the Bishop of Durham.

REFRESHMENTS:
There are several pubs, hotels and cafés in Bishop Auckland.
*The New Monkey*, Hunwick (tel no: 0388 450689).
*The Brown Trout,* Sunnybrow (tel no: 0388 746454).

# Walk 88    BRANDON TO BISHOP AUCKLAND    9$^1/_2$m (15km)

Maps: OS Sheets Landranger 88, 92 & 93; Pathfinder NZ 24/34, NZ 12/13 & NZ 23/33.

*Along the line of the Brandon to Bishop Auckland railway.*
Start: At 250415, the Broompark Picnic Area.
Finish: Newton Cap viaduct, Bishop Auckland.

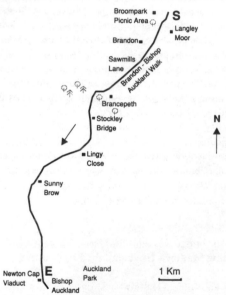

From Broompark Picnic Area descend to the River Deerness and cross it on a footbridge at a place where the line spanned it on a magnificent wooden viaduct. Continue southwards, passing playing fields that have been created on reclaimed pit heaps, and modern housing, to reach Sawmills Lane. The walk passes Brancepeth station to the west of the village and crosses Stockley Gill, just beyond it. The trackside bungalow at Stockley Bridge was originally a railway man's cottage. Soon the trees give way to views across the Wear Valley where, set among parkland, is Whitworth Hall, home of Bobby Shafto. Two farms close to the disused track to your left as you walk southward are, firstly, Ox Close, a name that suggests a medieval origin, and then Lingy Close, named when heather covered the nearby hills. Further away, to the south-

182

east, Kirk Merrington church can be seen. Because it is visible from almost anywhere in central Durham it was used by the Ordnance Survey as a triangulation point when they first mapped the county in 1856. As Willington comes nearer the walk becomes urban. Messrs. Straker and Love had their headquarters in Willington. They leased the collieries in the area and made their fortune from a process that used poor quality coal to make good quality coke.

The route returns to the countryside near Sunnybrow where there are some deep, wooded ravines. A mile south of Willington, at Roughlea, the walk makes a slight detour as a result of a missing bridge, but it is soon back on the trackbed again. It was near this section of the walk that shales and clay were dug for brickmaking. There were six brick works along a four mile stretch of the valley downstream of Hunwick. As Bishop Auckland is approached the valley floor to your left, which surrounds Flatts Farm, is a flat and fertile plain of silt deposited by the River Wear. Ahead, to the left of Bishop Auckland, is the Bishop's Palace, while the Town Hall is in the centre. Between you and the town Newton Cap viaduct spans the river and this is where the walk ends.

POINTS OF INTEREST:
The main reason for the railway line being built was to carry coal and coke. It was the brain child of George Hudson, the railway king, but his empire collapsed before the line was started.

REFRESHMENTS:
Hotels, pubs and cafés in Bishop Auckland.

Maps: OS Sheets Landranger 92; Outdoor Leisure 30.
*An interesting, but strenuous, walk along the County Durham/*
*North Yorkshire border.*
Start: Barningham village.

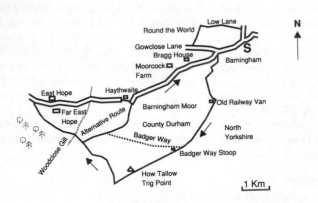

From Barningham village walk south-west. Where the road bends right, go left across a cattle grid and through a gate to continue on to the moor, along a track. Where this curves left, go straight ahead past a stone monument on your right. This was erected to mark an exceptionally large bag of grouse. It was once stolen, but found in North Wales and returned to its plinth. Cross a stream on a footbridge, climb steeply up the moor side and continue southwards on a good track to reach a gate in a wall near an old railway, to the left, Go right, across a ditch. Walk south-west, keeping close to the boundary wall on your left, passing first a boundary stone and, a little further on, a second stone wedged against the wall inscribed **Badger Way Stoop**. Continuing beside the wall, soon after a scar is climbed, the trig point on **How Tallon**, the highest point on the walk, is reached.

Soon after leaving How Tallon the wall gives way to a wire fence: keep with the fence until a metal gate in it is reached. There turn right along a track going roughly north-west, between shakeholes. When Osmaril Gill is reached keep to the west of it, heading towards Cross Gill, seen ahead. A little short of the Gill go north-west, on an undefined route aiming for The Stang Forest. Cross Woodclose Gill and climb to a gate into a forest showing the sign 'Black Hill Gate'. Go through and along a track to a yellow marker. Bear left, passing another yellow marker which directs you straight on to a forest gate on to the Hope Road. Turn right for $2^1/_2$ miles, passing Far East Hope, Haythwaite, Moorcock and Bragg House farms. When Scargill Road is reached turn left along it for almost $^1/_2$ mile to reach a lane on the right. Turn on to this, which will bring you, after $1^1/_2$ miles, back into Barningham village. This final 2 mile long section is well loved by the locals. It is known by them as the Walk Around the World, but nobody seems to know why.

## POINTS OF INTEREST:

**Badger Way Stoop** – Placed here long before the wall was built, the Badger Way Stoop could be seen on the horizon by 'badgers', pack horse train guides using the green road from Hill Top to Marske, to whom it was a welcome guide.

**How Tallon** – Although only 1467 feet above sea level the hill offers fine views of distant Pen Hill in Wensleydale, Great Shunner Fell, Great Whernside, The Stang, Cross Fell, Stainmore, Mickle Fell and the Cleveland Hills.

## REFRESHMENTS:

*The Millbank,* Barningham (tel no: 0833 21201).

# Walk 90   THE UPPER TEESDALE WATERFALLS   10m (16km)

Maps: OS Sheets Landranger 92; Outdoor Leisure 31.

*A moderate walk along field and riverside paths, but with some road walking.*

Start: Middleton-in-Teesdale car park.

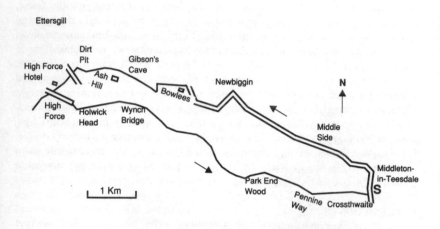

From the car park go left past a drinking fountain, cross Bridge Street and follow the B6277 along the Market Place. Keep on it until Hudeshope Beck is crossed. There continue straight ahead up steep road signposted 'Middleside'. Go along this quiet road – passing Lanehead, Middle Side, Bell and Ravelin farms – for 2 miles. At a road sign, turn left down steep Miry Lane into **Newbiggin** village. The panoramic views over Upper Teesdale from this 2 mile road section are excellent.

Follow the road behind Newbiggin, then go uphill to a stile, near a gate on your left, leading to a signposted path. Cross two waymarked fields, passing behind Hood Gill cottages, and continue along the edge of a field through a waymarked gate. Cross the middle of the next field and go down a track into Bowlees Picnic Area. Here make a short detour along a nature trail to see Summerhill Force pour over Gibson's Lane.

Leave the picnic area across Bowlees Beck and take the path for 100 yards to Bowlees Visitor Centre, a former chapel, which is worth a visit. Continue through a gate signposted as a public bridleway, and go uphill along what, until 1820, was the main road from Forest to Middleton. Ash Hill Cottage, which you pass on your left, offers more superb views and, once past it, the way is downhill to **Dirt Pit**. Cross Ettersgill Beck and turn left to the Ettersgill Road. Cross the road and go through a signposted stile into a field. Cross this and a second field. Go left, to High Force Hotel car park. Now comes a not to be missed detour, a pleasant woodland walk from opposite the hotel, upstream for $^1/_2$ mile to High Force, England's largest, and possibly finest, waterfall (see Note to Walk 24). The woodland belongs to the hotel and a small charge is made. From the hotel go left along the B6277 for $^1/_3$ mile, and then turn right down a lane marked 'Private Road – No Access for Vehicles', which is a public right of way. It leads to Holwick Head Bridge over the Tees, which you cross to join the Pennine Way. Anyone wishing to see High Force from a different viewpoint and without charge can turn right here and detour for $^1/_2$ mile upstream, skirting the gorge: the views are impressive and the thunder of falling water awe-inspiring. From Holwick Head Bridge go left, downstream, along the river bank, passing splendid Low Force, the Wynch Bridge (see Note to Walk 10) and, about $^1/_2$ mile further on, Scoberry Bridge. Continue to a ladder stile in a fence. Cross and bear left. Cross another stile and a footbridge over a feeder. Climb the wooded bank ahead and, at the top, turn left o continue across a muddy area, keeping close to a fence. At the end of the field cross a stile, then Unthank Beck, close to Park End Wood on your right. A Pennine Way sign in the next field directs you along a low wall and over a stile. Continue to a walled lane, The Old Holwick Road, and take it, following a clear path which skirts the Tees at one point, to the B6277. Turn left, passing the auction mart on your left. Cross Middleton Bridge and Middleton-in-Teesdale (see Note to Walk 5) will welcome you back after a most enjoyable walk.

## POINTS OF INTEREST:

**Newbiggin** – The Methodist Chapel, built in 1759, is the oldest in Methodism. John Wesley preached there and services have been held continuously ever since it was built.

**Dirt Pit** – The name derives from Deer Path. Rievaulx Abbey maintained a chapel at Dirt Pit for the forest keepers in the days when deer swarmed Teesdale Forest.

## REFRESHMENTS:

*The High Force Hotel* (tel no: 0833 22264).
Middleton-in-Teesdale has several pubs and hotels, a café and a fish shop.

Maps: OS Sheets Landranger 92; Outdoor Leisure 31.

*A walk along pleasant field and riverside paths, that becomes a bracing moor edge walk with extensive views of Weardale.*
Start: Wolsingham.

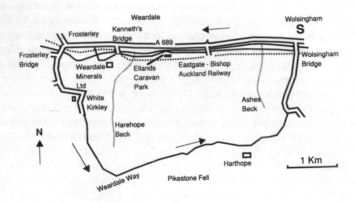

From Wolsingham go westwards along Front Street, turn left along the Causeway and cross the River Wear over Wolsingham Bridge. Continue along the road for 20 yards to where, at a footpath sign, you go through a gap in the wall on your right and down some steps to join a fenced path between the railway and the river. Go westwards along it, close to the railway, over Ashes Beck, across pastures and Hole Beck to reach the riverside. Continue upstream along the riverbank, crossing a feeder near a weir to exit, further on, near a road bridge. Continue along the same bank for ¹/₂ mile on a farm road signposted 'Landieu Farm'. Now enter a caravan park and continue upstream, leaving the river on a footbridge over Bollihope Beck. Take the field path ahead, following white waymarkers. Go through a gate on to a road. Turn left over a railway crossing, then right into the Broadwood plant of Weardale Minerals. Beyond the car park and some cabin offices, turn right at a footpath sign, cross a stile and climb a fenced and waymarked path through a wood overlooking the River Wear. Soon the narrow path bears right, through a waymarked gate, to the riverside. Cross the Wear on the wooden Kenneth's Bridge, and cross the railway line to enter Frosterly on an unmade road. Opposite the Frosterley Inn go left along the A689 to the west end of the village. Turn left down a lane signposted 'White Kirkley 1 mile' to re-cross the Wear on Frosterley Bridge. Go along the lane ahead for $1/_2$ mile to where, at a road junction on your right, the Wear Valley Way is joined. Continue along the lane, which bends left and crosses Bollihope Beck before entering White Kirkley. Stay on it as it climbs steadily through gates for over 1 mile, becoming unenclosed on the way. Just past Allotment House, a barn, it goes through a gate on to Pikestone Fell. Turn left along abroad track that edges the moor, past the **Elephant Trees** and continue eastwards for a further $1^1/_2$ miles to join the Hamsterley to Wolsingham road. Turn left along it, descending steep Wear Bank for $1^1/_2$ miles back into Wolsingham and the end of a grand walk.

## POINTS OF INTEREST:
**Elephant Trees** – The trees are so named because when seen from a distance they look like elephants crossing the skyline in single file, linked tail to trunk.

## REFRESHMENTS:
There are pubs and a café in Wolsingham.
*The Frosterley Inn,* Frosterley (tel no: 0388 527349).
*The Black Bull Inn,* Frosterley (tel no: 0388 527784).

**THE RIVER BALDER**                10m (16km)

Maps: OS Sheets Landranger 92; Outdoor Leisure 31.

*An exhilarating penetration of the High Pennine with superb views. Compass needed.*

Start: At 930188, the car park at the north end of the Balderhead Reservoir dam.

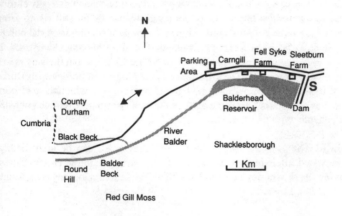

Leave the car park, going north to exit on to a minor road. Turn left to pass Sleetburn Farm on your left. Beyond are the derelict Primrose Hill, working Fell Syke, East and West Carngill and derelict Balderhead farms. About $^1/_4$ mile west of the last farm, where a gate straddles the road, there is a car park on the right. Continue through the gate along what has become a farm track with a green band along its middle. Goldsborough is on the horizon behind you and Shacklesborough is to your left. Soon a second gate is reached, close to a black fieldhouse on your right. Go through and continue ahead, ignoring the track to the right. The way descends into the head of a short side valley which is fenced off: enter through a metal gate. Cross the feeder, climb its far side and where the path divides go right, through a gate, back on to the moor. The way has now become a green track which at first bears slightly right, before veering left to follow a course parallel to the depression on your left along which the River Balder flows to reach the reservoir. When a shallow depression is reached, cross it and, after climbing the far side, turn left where the path divides and continue along a green track, still going parallel to the Balder on your left. Where the path splits again, on approaching a broken facing wall, take the left-hand fork, descending and going through a gap in the wall. Continue fairly steeply downhill along an indistinct path, aiming for the meeting of two becks just ahead. As a guide a waterfall and a sheepfold are clearly seen in the valley bottom. With the land falling away in front of you the path becomes clear again, and a footbridge with a handrail comes into view, crossing Black Beck, the right-hand of two becks. Cross this footbridge and continue along a steeply climbing track. On reaching the rim of the valley continue westwards on still rising ground close to a drainage ditch on your right, taking as a guide a small hut on the horizon. The track has now shrunk to a narrow ribbon and at times becomes indistinct. The ground ahead becomes marshy, especially close to Balder Beck, but the way is to the right of the low lying ground. The wire fence is the Cumbrian border with Durham and to get there you must cross a nice squelchy bit of ground on which the path comes and goes, adding to the fun. This is the apex of the walk. From here retrace your steps.

## POINTS OF INTEREST:
Looking westwards from the fence, the Eden Valley scarp can be identified, and Shacklesborough, with its cairn and trig point, is prominent on the eastern horizon. Lovely Pennine scenery is on all sides and the views on the return journey are absolutely stunning.

## REFRESHMENTS:
None en route, the nearest are the Hury Reservoir tea-rooms.

Walk 93    **KILLHOPE WHEEL AND ALLENHEADS**    10m (16km)
Maps: OS Sheets Landranger 87; Pathfinder NY 84/94.
*A strenuous route. It may be difficult to follow in mist, but on a
clear day the views are grand.*
Start: At 824433, the Killhope Wheel car park.

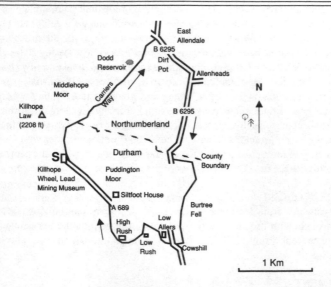

From the car park cross Killhope Burn, and then cross the A689 to a gate marked
'Weardale Estate – Private'. Enter Weardale Forest and take the track left northwards,
up Carriers Hill. Go over a stile at the end of the forest on to Middlethorpe Moor,
keeping to the left of a burn – all the becks are burns hereabouts. Continue northwards
to cross boundary (going out of County Durham into Northumberland) at a height of
2025 feet, the highest point of the walk. The summit of Killhope Law, 2208 feet, is
seen to the left, (westward), and the head of East Allendale is straight ahead (northward).
When a green bridleway is reached, continue along this very clear track for a good
mile, passing Dodd Reservoir on your left. Descend to the River East Allen, cross it
using Smelt Mill Bridge, and turn right along a quiet road, past some cottages, into
Dirt Pot (see Note to Walk 90). Here, a cascading waterfall, opposite Spring Cottage

192

Studio, catches the eye. Continue along the road, past a converted chapel which was once Dirt Pot's Youth Hostel, to reach Allenheads, 1400 feet above sea level and reputed to be the highest village in England. Leave this former lead mining centre by turning right, along the B6295, just past the Post Office. Stay on the road for a mile, climbing to the County boundary. There, turn left over a fence and follow the boundary wall-cum-fence on your right for $^1/_2$ mile across moorland. At a gate, turn right and go south along a bridleway across Burtree Fell for $1^1/_2$ miles into Cowshill. From the village go right, past the church, along a minor road to reach the A689. Go right, along the main road to a footpath sign opposite three cottages. Turn left through a gate and go down a track to cross Killhope Burn by Low Allers Bridge. Turn right between farmhouses, and go along an enclosed track. Continue across three meadows and descend diagonally to Heathery Bridge, which has two waymarkers. Do not cross. Instead, go along the track, leftwards (westwards) to Blakeley Field. Take the track to Killhope Burn, cross it by bridge and climb the green track to reach the A689 almost opposite Slit Foot House. turn left for $^1/_2$ mile to return to the car park at **Killhope Wheel**.

## POINTS OF INTEREST:

**Killhope Wheel** – Restoration work is continuing at Killhope Wheel, which is now a lead mining museum with working models and audio visual displays. Smithy, stables and miners' lodgings have all been restored and the authorities hope that the Park Level Lead Crushing Mill, with its 34 feet high water wheel – the Killhope Wheel – will be fully operational in the near future. Killhope is, without doubt, the best preserved lead mining site in the North Pennines.

## REFRESHMENTS:

*The Allenheads Inn,* Allenheads (tel no: 0434 85200).
*The Cowshill Hotel,* Cowshill (tel no: 0388 537236).
*Craft shop and tea room,* Allenheads.

# Walk 94   ROOKHOPE AND REDBURN COMMON   10m (16km)

Maps: OS Sheets Landranger 87; Pathfinder NY 84/94.

*A strenuous, but really glorious, walk.*

Start: At 940428, Rookhope.

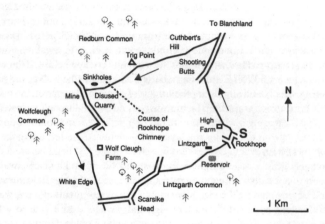

Cross the bridge outside Rookhope Inn and immediately turn right at a footpath sign to climb a steep lane past some houses, close to a wall on your left. Go through a kissing gate and on through a facing white gate. Mid-way between that gate and a farmhouse, take the track on your right to enter open pasture through a gate. Go diagonally left on a bearing of 335°, aiming for the corner post of a paddock, and continue along a faint meandering track. On your right is a gill which is crossed near its head by the Blanchland Road: once the road's black and white markers are seen, aim for them. Turn right along the road for 1 mile, crossing a cattle grid and passing butts and a lay-by. Just before a stile on your right, turn left along a faint track which soon becomes more distinct and easier to follow. The track soon descends to cross a syke and continues through deep heather, waymarked with posts set at intervals. This is Cuthbert's Hill. Walk on a bearing of 247°, aiming for a gate in a facing fence. Go through and continue, gradually drawing close to a fence on the left. When the track vanishes, stay close to the fence to reach a point where, left of a trig point, four fences meet. The going is strenuous, but the views panoramic on this section. Go through a gate at the four fence corner and walk on a bearing of 233°, through the heather, to cross the line of Rookhope smelt mill chimney near its top. Now descend past a disused quarry and to the left of several fenced off sink holes to reach a track leading to the road below. Turn right, briefly, then go left to reach a **working mine** area. Go through, keeping to the left bank of Rookhope Beck, passing buildings and winding gear, to exit through a gate and along a clear track. Continue to a T-junction. Turn right, bridge Rookhope Beck, pass a ruin and follow a meandering track across moorland. Where the track goes left in to a meadow, continue uphill, close to a wall on your left. Just beyond the second pasture on your left, turn left and continue close to the wall (it is still on your left), with Wolf Cleugh Farm below. At a gate in the wall go diagonally uphill, climbing steeply and aiming for the largest of three spoil heaps on the horizon. Go past the heap to reach a gate in a facing wall but do not go through it. Instead, go left to facing wall, crossing it where the wire has been removed, and continue downhill to exit through a gate on to a minor road near a T-junction. Turn left along the road, going uphill over its brow and down the other side. At the last bend before a copse, where a stream edges the road's right side, cross the stream and a nearby wall, just below a fence: this is a right of way, despite appearances. Cross the field ahead on a bearing of 80°. In the next field go slightly right to reach the remains of a gateway. Go through and contour left, past a ruin, crossing the next field to a gate in a fence. Continue down the next field, using Rookhope incline as a guide. Go through a gate left of a reservoir and, bearing left, descend to a derelict farm. Cross the stile on your right and follow a clear track down hill back into Rookhope.

## POINTS OF INTEREST:

**Working Mine** – Fluorspar and a little lead is mined by Wearside Minerals beside Rookhope Burn. The main shaft is 480 feet deep and links with a drift entrance further up the valley that goes underground at a gradient of 1 in 4. Once used as a welding flux, fluorspar is today used in many ways, including the manufacture of ceramics. Curlews, golden plover and pheasants are just a few samples of the varied bird life encountered on this splendid walk.

## REFRESHMENTS:

*The Rookhope Inn,* Rookhope (tel no: 0388 517215).

Walk 95    **THE DERWENT RAILWAY**    10¹/₂m (17km)
Maps: OS Sheets Landranger 88; Pathfinder NZ 05/15, NZ 06/
16 & NZ 26/36.
*An interesting all-seasons walk.*
Start: At 200621, Swalwell Station Visitor Centre, Swalwell.
Finish: At 100519, Blackhill, near Consett.

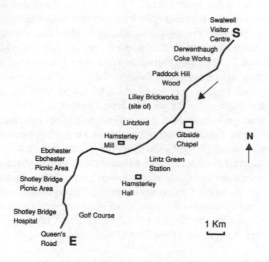

Leave the Visitor Centre along the disused Derwent railway line, westwards, passing, after ¹/₂ mile, the site of Derwenthaugh coke works. This is being reclaimed, hopefully to allow the natural beauty of the valley to be extended. Axwell Hall, which overlooks the valley to the north, was built by the Claverings, who were colliery owners. Soon Thornley Wood is passed, on the right: it contains a Woodlands' Centre which is the starting point for two nature trails. In just over 1 mile a path leads away, left, to Old Hollinside, a 13th century fortified house. The surrounding woodland is part of the Derwent Walk Country Parkland. As the old line continues up the valley the ruins of Gibside Hall which was built in 1620, are clearly seen. The nearby 140 feet high monument was built in 1750 to decorate Gibside's grounds. Gibside chapel, a little

196

further on, has been restored by the National Trust and is open to the public. Lilley brickworks, the site of which is near and to the north of Rowlands Gill, was famed for its distinctive off-white brick, which was made from clay from a nearby railway cutting. Hamsterley viaduct, crossed later in the walk, is built of Lilley bricks. From the site of the brickworks continue close to the A694 on your right and where it curves right, go left, briefly, along the B6314, then right to cross the railway viaduct over the River Derwent. Continue along the trackbed, passing Friarside chapel on your right, and soon reaching Lintz Green Station, from where an interesting detour leads to **Lintzford**.

From the two viaducts beyond Lintz Green Station there are bird's eye views of the tree tops in the valley below. Hamsterley Mill, to the north as the line begins to curve towards Ebchester is now a prestigious commuter suburb. About 1 mile beyond **Ebchester**, Shotley Bridge is reached. The next two bridges are now gone, and the line goes between Shotley Bridge Hospital on the right and a golf course on the left. It is then only a short walk into Blackhill.

POINTS OF INTEREST:

**Lintzford** – In 1649 a corn mill was built at the village: it later became a papermill and, in 1922, an ink works. Lintzford House and the bridge are both 18th century and are very attractive.

**Ebchester** – The bells of Ebchester Church strike the quarter hour, and on special occasions ring out hymn tunes to call parishioners to worship. The church is partly built of 'second-hand' stone from the ramparts of Vindomora, the Roman fort on which Ebchester was built.

# Walk 96  SUNDERLAND BRIDGE AND WHITWORTH ROAD    11m (17.5km)

Maps: OS Sheets Landranger 93; Pathfinder NZ 23/33.

*A moderately easy walk through peaceful Durham countryside.*

Start: At 265377, Sunderland Bridge.

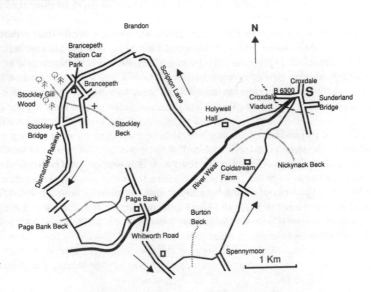

From the north end of Sunderland Bridge, an old, four-arched road bridge over the River Wear, go left along a path signposted 'Brancepeth – Bridle Path Only' which goes under the nearby, eleven-arched Croxdale Viaduct and then uphill for $^1/_2$ mile to Holywell Hall. Turn left and continue, still going uphill, for a further $^1/_2$ mile to Scripton Lane. Turn right along it for a good mile to reach the A690. Cross and go through a gate opposite. Go straight ahead to the disused Brandon to Bishop Auckland railway line, now a popular railway walk. Turn left along the trackbed, passing Brancepeth Station after $1^1/_2$ miles, and going across well-wooded Stockley Gill. About $1^1/_2$ miles further on, on the approach to Willington Industrial Estate, go through a gap in the fence on your left, close to a bench, and take an unsignposted track to the A690. Cross and turn left along the road for 30 yards, then go down an unsignposted lane on the

198

right. Pass, on your left, Willington's old brick works and tip with, beyond, an ugly group of buildings. At a junction of lanes beyond this group there is a choice of routes. One way is through a facing gate and along the edge of a field to the River Wear and left along the river bank to join Whitworth Lane at Page Bank Bridge. The alternative is to go left through a metal gate and along a byway for $1^1/_2$ miles. Where the track divides, turn left and go up a steep hill past a terrace of four cottages called Page Bank East. This will bring you to Whitworth Lane. Turn right along it to Page Bank to meet the first route.

Cross the River Wear on Page Bank Bridge and continue along Whitworth Road. After $^1/_2$ mile Whitworth Hall (see Note to Walk 87) is reached on your left. Just beyond the entrance to Whitworth Hall Garden, turn left through a signposted kissing gate and go through a group of trees, keeping close to a high wall at first, then a fence on your left. Go out through another kissing gate, turn right and right again to a fenced path. Go along it past a line of small oaks and through two more kissing gates into narrow Black Wood Plantation. Continue through the wood along a surfaced lane and go eastwards along another lane, skirting a new Spennymoor housing estate and the Rosa Shafto Nature Reserve, into Valley Burn. Cross the burn on a footbridge, climb out of the valley – leaving it at a sewage works entrance – and continue along a country lane. At a crossroads, turn left and after a few yards cross a stile beside a gate on the right and go along a fenced path. Continue northwards, crossing stiled fields and, where a cart track from Coldstream Farm is joined, go right for a few yards, then left along the edge of a field into Coldstream Wood. Take the muddy woodland footpath and descend steeply out of the wood to cross Nickynack Beck on a footbridge. Take the beckside path, with the wood on your right, to join a riverside path which will bring you back under Croxdale Viaduct, past another sewage works, and so back to Sunderland Bridge.

POINTS OF INTEREST:
In 1635, 1400 trees were felled in Stockley Gill Wood to build Britain's first three-decker warship at Woolwich.

REFRESHMENTS:
Sandwiches are the order of the day on this walk, there being neither pub nor café along the route.

# Walk 97   THE DEERNESS AND LANCHESTER VALLEYS   11m (17.5km)

Maps: OS Sheets Landranger 88; Pathfinder NZ 04/14 & 24/34.

*This walk, along two reclaimed railway lines, linked by field paths, offers extensive views of the Mid-Durham countryside.*

Start: At 250415, the Broompark Picnic Area.

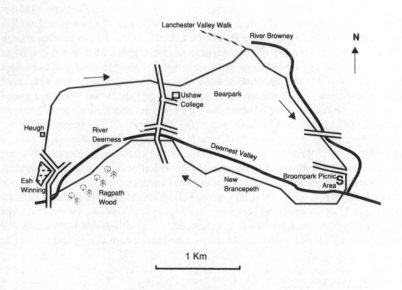

From the Picnic Area follow the direction indicated by the signpost to 'Ushaw Moor – 1¾ miles', to reach the eastern end of the Deerness Valley Walk which follows the course of the former **Deerness Valley railway** line. Go westwards along the track bed, with the River Deerness below and on the left. Just beyond the former Ushaw Moor railway station, now a private dwelling, the way leads downhill and crosses a road to a car park. It next crosses the River Deerness on a concrete bridge and climbs beside a plantation to regain the railway's original level. While the railway was operating this shallow valley was spanned by a wooden trestle viaduct. At this point, New Brancepeth is to your left (south) and Ushaw Moor to your right (north). Continue along the disused line to Esh Winning, where you take any of the exits, right, into the village, and go through it to reach the B6302. Turn left along this road to just beyond a Catholic church. Turn right along a track going northwards to a stile. Cross and climb the field ahead as far as a stile on the right. Cross and turn left up a field, staying close to a fence on your left. At the top of the field cross a waymarked stile and follow an enclosed track to Heugh Farm. Go through the farmyard, passing the farmhouse on your left, and continue up the track ahead. Beyond the third stile the track bifurcates: take the right-hand way, curving eastwards, along the top of three gated fields. Pass Esh Hall and go along a farm road which passes the front of Low Esh Farm. At the Langley Park-Bearpark road turn right for about 80 yards to reach a sign, 'Ushaw College – Goods Entrance'. Turn left along a signposted road to the back of the college. Bear left through a wood, then left along a lane to cross a stile near a house. Go straight ahead, over another stile, turn right, down the edge of a field, and exit through a rusty gate on your right. Now go along a track that edges the next three fields, then cross a stile and continue diagonally down the field ahead to reach the **Lanchester Valley Walk**, another disused railway line. Turn right down the Walk, leaving it briefly to cross the Bearpark-Durham road. On returning to the disused line, stay on the track bed for the final $1^1/_2$ miles back to the Broompark Picnic Area.

POINTS OF INTEREST:
**Deerness Valley railway** – The line opened in 1858 and closed in 1951. It was built to carry coal from Waterhouse colliery out of the valley.
**Lanchester Valley Walk** – The railway line opened on 1 September 1862 and closed 20 June 1966. It was first built as a single track to carry iron ore to Consett, but later it was doubled from Broompark to Lanchester to cater for coal traffic from Langley Park. The Walk along the old line was opened and is maintained by Durham County Council.
The tell-tale colliery blemishes, the pit heaps and other ugly coalmining eyesores in this area have been swept away by an ambitious land reclamation programme.

REFRESHMENTS:
There are pubs in Ushaw Moor and Esh Winning.

# Walk 98        THE VALE OF HARWOOD        11m (17.5km)

Maps: OS Sheets Landranger 92; Outdoor Leisure 31.

*A superb exploration of Harwood Gill and the wild moorland at the head of Teesdale.*

Start: At 854310, the Langdon Beck Hotel.

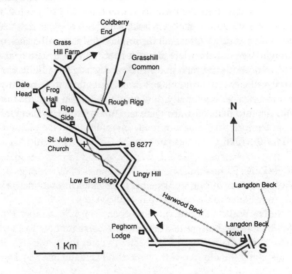

From the hotel go along the minor road, with Langdon Beck on your left. Cross Harwood Beck a little upstream of the confluence of the waters. Continue westwards for 1½ miles and turn right along a narrow, metalled road, passing, on your left, Reghorn Lodge. The road leads northwards past, firstly, Unthank Farm on the right, then Binks House and Marches Gill Farms on the left. The Harwood Valley is entered about 1 mile from the start of the road. As Lowend Bridge is approached, turn left, through a gate, and go upstream, close to the beck on your right, to a footbridge. Cross and continue past two decaying buildings, the Church of Saint Jude and an adjoining school. Keep ahead on a cart track leading uphill from the beck to Rigg Side Farm – once a shooting lodge of the Duke of Cleveland. There, turn left along a narrow lane to Herdship Farm, looked upon as the centre of the scattered hamlet of

Harwood. Continue along the lane, north-westwards, for a further $^1/_2$ mile, then turn right, past Frog Hall, and go up a gully to the next farm, Dale Head with its fine views across the valley to Cross Fell. Turn right at Dale Head and walk close to a wall on your left to reach deep-sided Ashgill. Cross to reach the site of Lady Rake Lead Mines of which the shaft opening and the engine bends are about all that remain. A short climb will bring you to the B6277, the Alston to Middleton-in-Teesdale road. Cross and go straight ahead, along a track, towards ruinous **Grass Hill Farm**. Just short of it the track bifurcates: take the right fork, climbing for 1 mile up Coldberry End. On approaching the summit of the track look for a path on your right, roughly going in a southerly direction down Grasshill Common. This path will bring you back to the B6277 at Rough Rigg, where it crosses a feeder. Turn right, along the road for $^1/_2$ mile, and then turn left on to a path going diagonally left, downhill, to join the narrow lane crossed on the outward journey – but at a different point. Turn left along the lane as far as the first junction on your right and go along that, down to the Lowend Bridge, beyond which you rejoin the outward route and follow it back to Langdon Beck Hotel.

## POINTS OF INTEREST:

**Grass Hill Farm** – When occupied this was the highest farm in Teesdale. Abandoned now to sheltering sheep, moaning winds and the ghosts of hill farmers defeated by the elements, it gazes across the valley, its empty windows like sightless eyes.

## REFRESHMENTS:

*The Langdon Beck Hotel,* Forest-in-Teesdale (tel no: 0833 22267).

# Walk 99     CRONKLEY FELL     12m (19km)

Maps: OS Sheets Landranger 92; Outdoor Leisure 31.

*Easy walking through one of the most interesting areas,*
*botanically and geologically, in England.*

Start: At 904271, Holwick village.

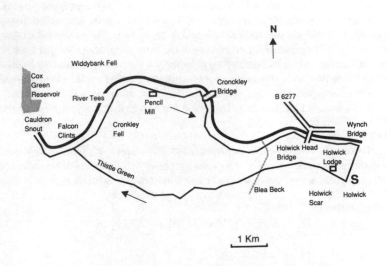

From the west end of Holwick take the bridleway uphill on to the moors, with Holwick Scar on the left and **Holwick Lodge** on the right. Follow the bridleway for $1^1/_2$ miles to where a signpost indicates a faint green track going due west across the moor. Take this, soon crossing Blea Beck and seeing White Force, a waterfall, on the left. Go uphill to the summit of Cronkley Fell, following the cairns: from the summit Birkdale Farm and Cow Green Reservoir can be seen. Now follow a green track down to the River Tees. Turn left, upstream, when you reach it for an exciting detour to visit Maize Beck where it flows into the Tees at the foot of Cauldron Snout (see Note to Walk 78). From this confluence of Maize Beck and the infant Tees, which is born to the west of Cow Green Reservoir on the eastern slopes of Cross Fell, retrace your steps to where, on the outward journey, you reached the Tees, and continue downstream, following the footpath along the foot of Cronkley Scar. Keep on this path, passing, after 2 miles, the remains of an old slate pencil mill, to Cronkley Bridge, where the Pennine Way is joined. Turn right along the farm road to Cronkley Farm. Keeping the farm buildings on your left, continue along a defined path to the end of the field ahead. Go left, then right, and climb through a gap in some crags, between juniper bushes. Go left and around two sides of a wire fence to reach a stile in a wall. Cross and go half-left, again on a clear path, through juniper bushes to return to the riverside. Keep on the riverside path, crossing three feeders on bridges, and passing, on your right, Blea Beck Force, an interesting waterfall. The path, now well-defined, passes High Force (see Note to Walk 24) and drops down to Holwick Head Bridge. Keeping on the same side of the river, continue downstream along the river bank to the Wynch Bridge, a fine suspension bridge across the Tees at Low Force (see Note to Walk 10). From the bridge turn right along a clear route across fields to Holwick and the end of a glorious walk.

POINTS OF INTEREST:
**Holwick Lodge** – The Lodge is the Earl of Strathmore's shooting lodge.
Rare plants grow on the sugar limestone which outcrops in the Whin Sill through which this walk winds.

REFRESHMENTS:
*The High Force Hotel* (tel no: 0833 22264).

# Walk 100 STANHOPE, EASTGATE AND ROOKHOPE 13m (21km)

Maps: OS Sheets Landranger 87 & 92; Pathfinder NY 84/94 and Outdoor Leisure 31.

*A good mix of low level riverside walking and high level walking.*

Start: Stanhope Market Place.

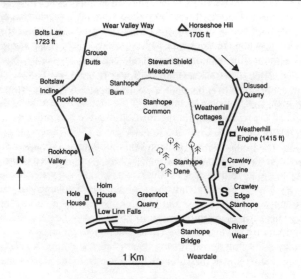

Leave Stanhope along the A689 and turn left down the B6278, opposite Stanhope Hall, to where Stanhope Bridge spans the River Wear. Do not cross: instead turn right, through a gate, and go along a track, passing, on your right, disused Greenfoot Quarry. Beyond the quarry, bear left, crossing firstly a stile, then a railway line to enter a meadow over a second stile. Turn right and walk upstream, westwards, for $2^1/_2$ miles. When Hag Bridge Caravan Park is reached, enter it through a wooden gate, and where the track goes through a gateway turn left along a wall side path to exit over a stile at the end of Hag Bank Bridge. Turn right along the road to reach the A689. Turn left into **Eastgate** and, at Cuthbert Bainbridge Memorial Chapel, turn right along a lane. Here a short diversion – going left at Rose Cottage, then right behind another cottage – will reward you with a good view of Low Linn Falls, a horseshoe

206

cascade. Return to the start of the diversion, and continue northwards, climbing steeply. Once past Holme House, on your right, the lane deteriorates into a track which will bring you to Hole House. There go through the right-hand of two gates and up Ashy Bank. At the top go through a gate and turn left along a contour overlooking wooded Rookhope Burn. Keeping close to a fence at first, the path soon forks left, downhill, to Rookhope Burn. Turn right by some gateposts and continue northwards climbing above the wooded valley and returning to the burn. Cross a feeder on a footbridge and continue upstream close to Rookhope Burn on your left, passing some ruinous buildings and old, fenced shafts. Soon after passing a capped, disused shaft, cross Rookhope Burn on a footbridge to join the Rookhope to Eastgate road. Turn right along it for 1 mile to reach Rookhope village, a one-time mining centre. Opposite the Post Office turn right along an unsurfaced track signposted 'Leading to Hylton Terrace', passing some garages on your left. Where the path splits, bear left, through a gate on to open moorland at the bottom of Boltslaw Incline. Climb the incline to the ruins of **Boltslaw Engine Works** and cottages. Keep on the disused line for four miles as it curves round the high side of Stanhope Common to reach the B6278. Turn right along this unfenced road for 1 mile to Weatherhill Cottages on your right and Weatherhill Engine on your left. Continue downhill parallel to the B6278 along the track bed of the disused Stanhope and Tyne Valley Railway for $1^1/_2$ miles to a partially renovated house on the site of the Crawley Engine. There, go left along a track. Once through gateposts, turn right by the garden wall of the house and keep on the path as it curves left along Crawley Edge. Where it forks right keep on it, going down the edge towards two kissing gates and bearing left over a stile. Go across two girder bridges over a large quarry, and continue downhill into an enclosed path which leads into Stanhope. Now go left, first along Chapel Street, then along Church Street, to the Market Place.

POINTS OF INTEREST:
**Eastgate** – The village once marked the boundary of the Bishop of Durham's deer park. Near the public telephone there is a replica of a Roman altar, the original of which was found in Rookhope Burn on 15th November 1869. It was dedicated to the god Silvanus and is dated at AD 238 – 244.
**Boltslaw Engine Works** – The disused railway serving the Engine Works, and the mines around Rookhope, was the highest standard gauge railway built in the UK.

REFRESHMENTS:
There are hotels, pubs and cafés in Stanhope.
*The Rookhope Inn,* Rookhope (tel no: 0388 517215).
*The Cross Keys,* Eastgate (tel no: 0388 517234).